ALLIGATOR at the AIRPORT

A Language Activities Dictionary

Kaye Wiley and Ethel Berger

Addison-Wesley Publishing Company, Inc.

A Publication of the ESL Publishing Group
Product Development Director: Judith M. Bittinger
Executive Editor: Elinor Chamas
Editorial Development: Clare Siska
Production/Manufacturing: James W. Gibbons
Cover/Text Design and Production: Emily Sper
Cover Art: Ethel Berger

Acknowledgments

Special thanks to all the children whose original dictionaries inspired this book, especially to Asuka Onuma, who permitted us to adapt her dictionary drawings as guide words on the letter pages. Grateful acknowledgment is also made to the faculty and staff of Hamden Hall School for their support, and to the many young artists and authors whose ideas and imaginations helped bring *Alligator* to life.

...And to our families who helped us arrive *at the Airport* with *Alligator:* Jim Maggart, Eric Berger, Stephanie Johnson, Philip Johnson, Aylin Maggart, Michael Maggart, Timothy Berger and Lolly Berger, Carol Wiley, Gail Wiley, and Edith Wiley.

...And to our colleagues and friends: Judith Bittinger, head of the ESL team at Addison-Wesley; Clare Siska and Elinor Chamas, our editors; also to Lanse Crane, Klaus Gemming, Gretchen Lytle, Jim Davidson, Dorie Baker, George Colburn, Margaret Klimentidis, Sally McCandless, Patricia Garland, Nathan Garland, Sally Wood, Lucille Hogan, Jane Hedges, Susan Broshjeit, Jacqueline Jewett, Kathy Prout, Brenda Stabell, Lenox Reed, Donna Ogle, and Nancy Rupp.

Printed in the United States of America.
ISBN: 0-201-58818-8
7 8 9 10 VG 97

Preface

Alligator at the Airport is a language activities dictionary for beginning readers and young students of English as a Second Language. Designed in the spirit of Whole Language, it is based on the idea that children learn vocabulary and initial sounds most effectively when they are actively engaged and having fun.

There are more than 1,000 illustrated high-frequency words in ***Alligator at the Airport***. It can be used as a supplement to a standard children's dictionary, such as ***The Addison Wesley Picture Dictionary***, or as a separate language activities book. The detailed illustrations are easy for students of all languages to understand.

Each of the twenty-six alphabet scenes includes 20-60 essential words, which are embedded in the scene according to first letter — for example, an **a**pple, an **a**rtist, and an **a**stronaut are all **a**t the **a**irport. The activities following these scenes are arranged in alphabetical sequence — i.e., **A**: **A**ddress, **A**ge, **A**nimals — and have instructions that also stress initial letters — i.e., **F**inish the **f**ace; **M**ake a **m**ap. The activity pages are large and open-ended, with humorous pictures and creative suggestions that encourage children to talk, draw, and write freely.

Alligator at the Airport helps students learn to:

1. name and label objects,
2. practice beginning sounds,
3. classify words,
4. alphabetize,
5. make lists,
6. use a reference,
7. use directional words,
8. infer differences,
9. predict outcomes, and
10. engage in cooperative language learning.

The pages feature simple directions for teachers, but students can feel free to explore whatever activities interest them. Each letter section begins with a pair of pages — an alphabetical scene and a letter page — enabling students to proceed without instruction once they understand the pattern. Front pages have been specifically designed to include survival vocabulary for ESL students, i.e., address, telephone number, counting, days of the week; for this reason beginning English speakers may wish to begin with *A* and proceed alphabetically. Students who wish to start their dictionary with the first letter of their own name are welcome to do so.

Hidden in the letter scenes of ***Alligator at the Airport*** are special symbols for students to discover. These are whimsical characters created to inspire conversation and pose challenges:

Alphabet Animals
(Try to find them!)

Verb People
(What are they doing?)

The verb people, like other illustrations, are coded in the Dictionary Word List at the back of the book, but they have many possible interpretations: for example, the *D* figure above could be either **d**rinking or **d**raining the glass — or **d**igesting a **d**rink! (All are possible *D* verbs.) The Word List is simply a guide. ***Alligator at the Airport*** has many "right" answers to its activities — as many as its young authors and artists can imagine.

After students have completed the activity pages of ***Alligator at the Airport***, they can continue to add words to the letter pages from their outside reading. In this way their personalized dictionary becomes an ongoing reference and a companion as they "take off" into reading and writing.

CONTENTS and CONCEPTS

Practice writing the **A**lphabet from **A** to **Z**. Say the letters or sing them.

AaBbCcDdEeFfGgHhIiJjKkLlMmNnOoPpQqRrSsTtUuVvWwXxYyZz

AaBbCcDdEeFfGgHhIiJjKkLlMmNnOoPpQqRrSsTtUuVvWwXxYyZz

AaBbCcDdEeFfGgHhIiJjKkLlMmNnOoPpQqRrSsTtUuVvWwXxYyZz

A

Aa Bb Cc Dd Ee Ff Gg Hh Ii Jj Kk Ll Mm Nn Oo Pp Qq Rr Ss Tt Uu Vv Ww Xx Yy Zz

Say the numbers from **1-20** and write them.

______ **1** one	______ **6** six	______ **11** eleven	______ **16** sixteen
______ **2** two	______ **7** seven	______ **12** twelve	______ **17** seventeen
______ **3** three	______ **8** eight	______ **13** thirteen	______ **18** eighteen
______ **4** four	______ **9** nine	______ **14** fourteen	______ **19** nineteen
______ **5** five	______ **10** ten	______ **15** fifteen	______ **20** twenty

My Dictionary

by

(author's name)

(class)

(year)

ALLIGATOR at the AIRPORT

Are you able to find the ***A*** *alphabet animal?*

Say the A words and color them.

Put a ✔ by these A words when you find the pictures.

✔alligator	___ask	___animal	___ant	___apple
___alphabet	___ambulance	___airplane	___aquarium	___artist

Aa

More A words that I found:

airport

My A Page

ant

Draw or paste some pictures of **A** words here. Label your pictures.

My Address

Airmail

name

address

city or town

state zip code

My age is __________.

My area code + telephone number is:

(___ ___ ___) ___ ___ ___ - ___ ___ ___ ___

Apples **around** Boxes

Draw **an** apple . . .

...rolling **across** the box

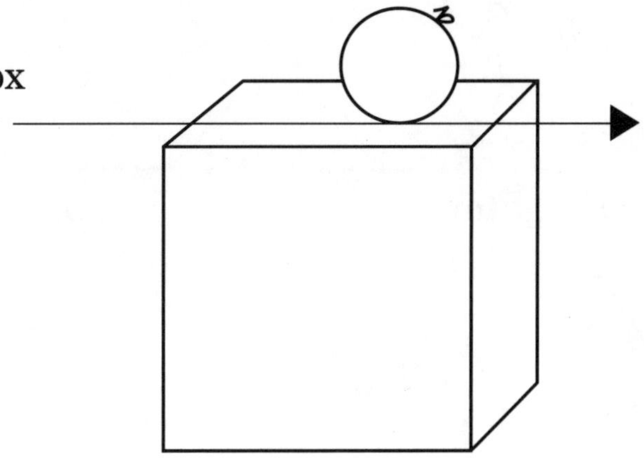

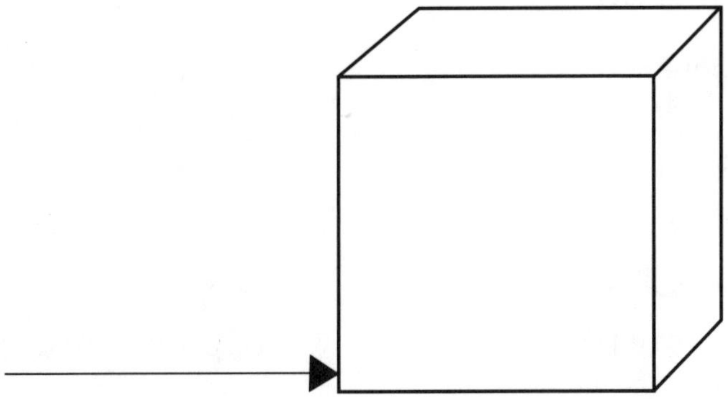

...leaning **against** the box

...floating **above** the box

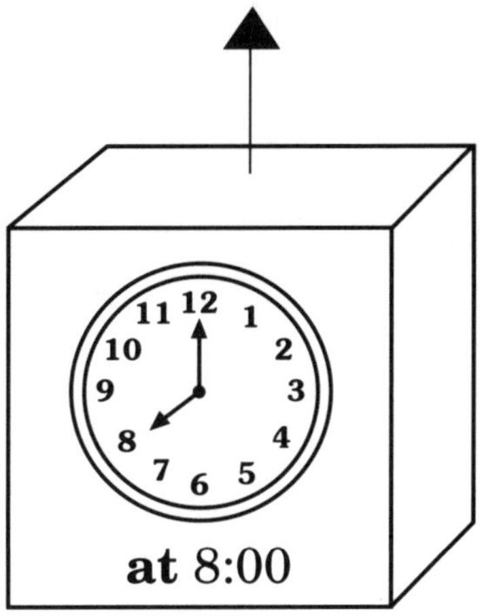

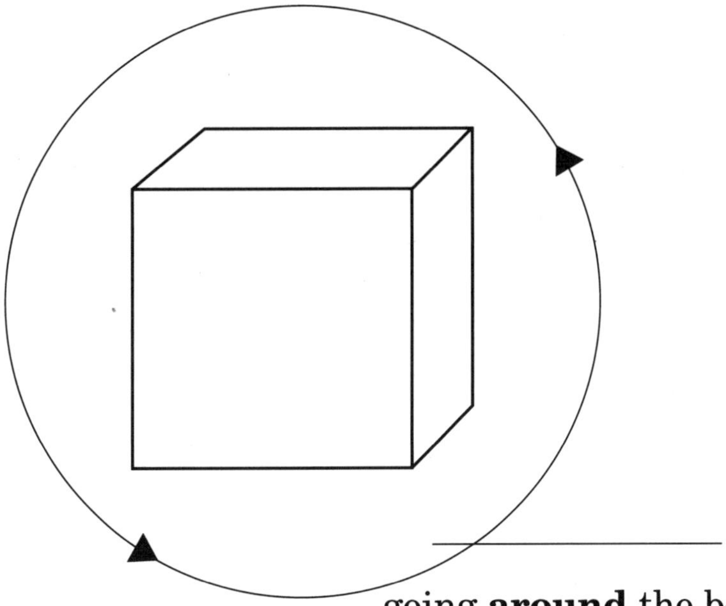

...going **around** the box

...rolling **along** the road

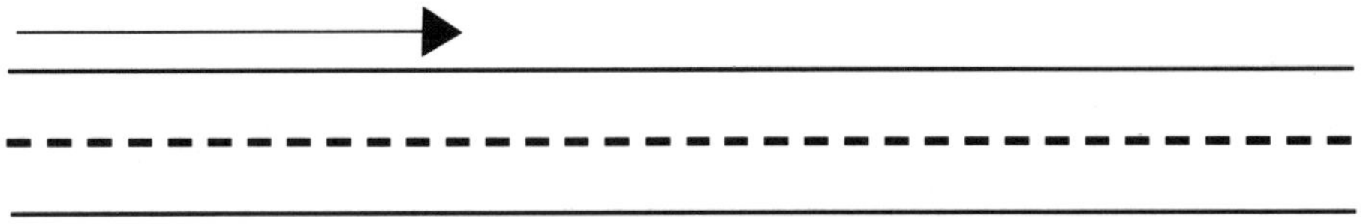

Animals

Here **a**re some of the **a**nimals in this book. (Circle) your favorite **a**nimals.

alligator

bear

cat

dragon

elephant

fox

gorilla

hippopotamus

iguana

jellyfish

kangaroo

lion

mouse

owl

pig

quail

rabbit

seal

tiger

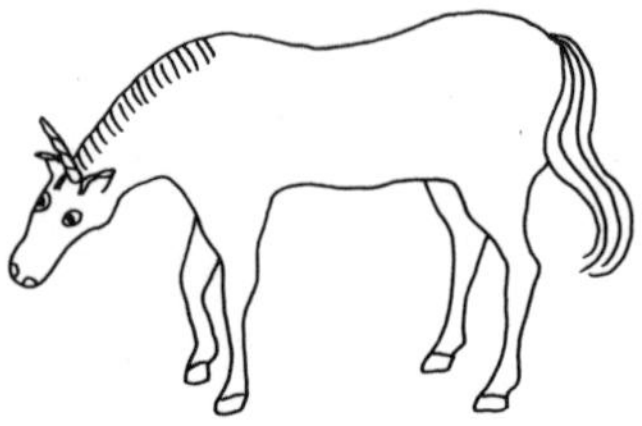

unicorn

vulture

wolf

yak

zebra

Another **A**nimal

Draw **a**nother **a**nimal that you like.

Write **a**bout your **a**nimal.

____

____

*I **a**m **a**n **a**rtist too.*

BEAR in the BEDROOM

*Be sure to find the **B** alphabet animal.*

Say the B words and color them.

Put a ✔ by these B words when you find the pictures.

___ball	___bed	___boy	___book	___bus
___baby	___bird	___blackboard	___boat	___bread

Bb

More B words that I found:

My B Page

Draw or paste some pictures of **B** words here. Label your pictures.

The Body

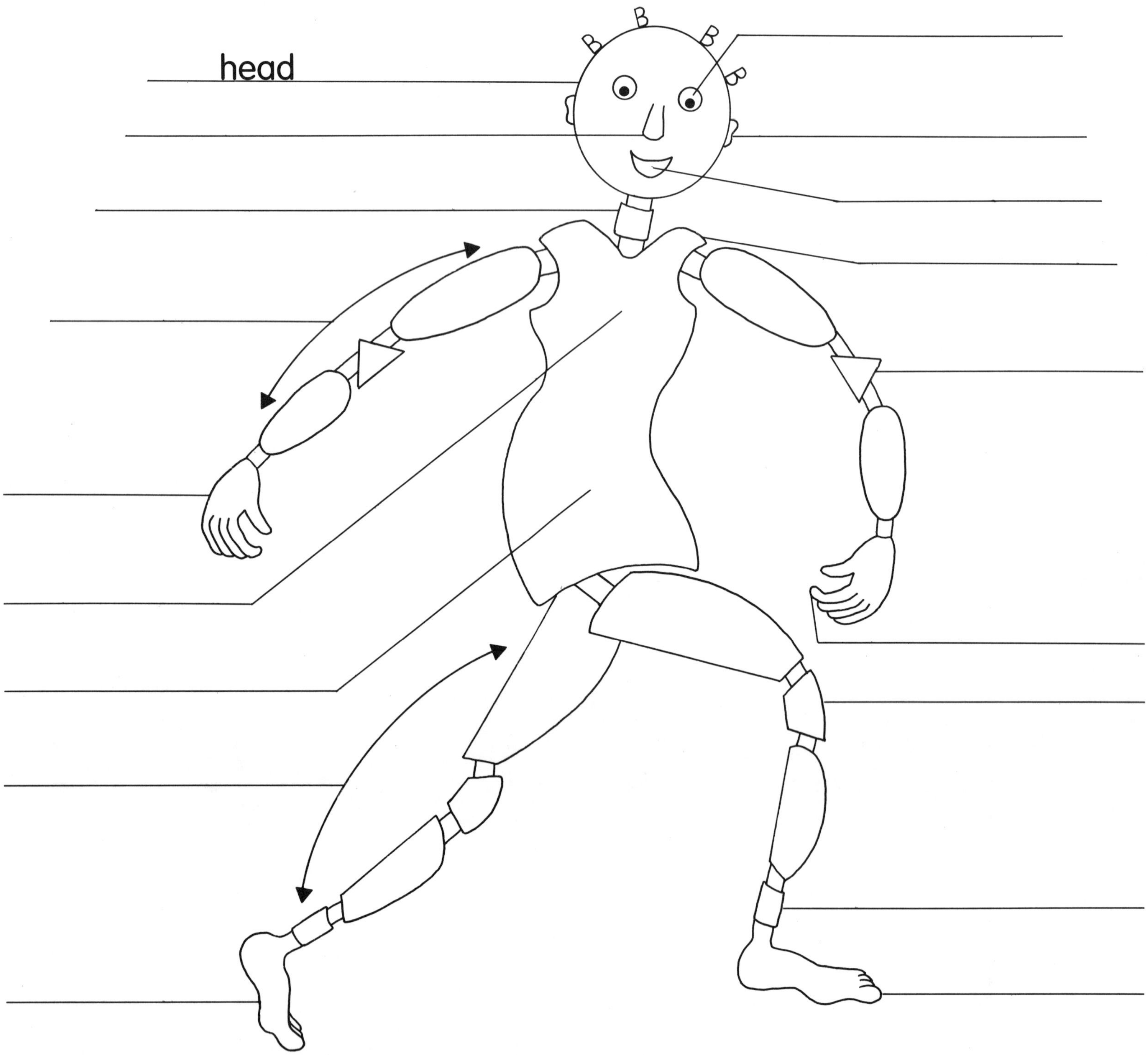

Label the parts of the **b**ody.

___toe	___shoulder	___finger	___knee	___ankle	___mouth
___arm	✔head	___hand	___leg	___eye	___elbow
___nose	___foot	___stomach	___ear	___neck	___chest

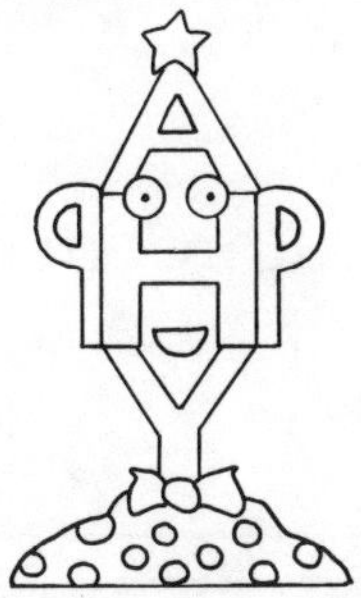

Birthday

Draw a **b**irthday party or celebration.

Birthday

	Yes	No
Is there a **b**irthday cake in your picture?	______	______
Are there **b**alloons in your picture?	______	______
Do you know the song "Happy **B**irthday to You?"	______	______

Bedroom and Bathroom

Circle the things that go in a **b**edroom. Put a ✔ **b**y the things that go in a **b**athroom.
Use **b**oth marks for things that can go in **b**oth rooms.

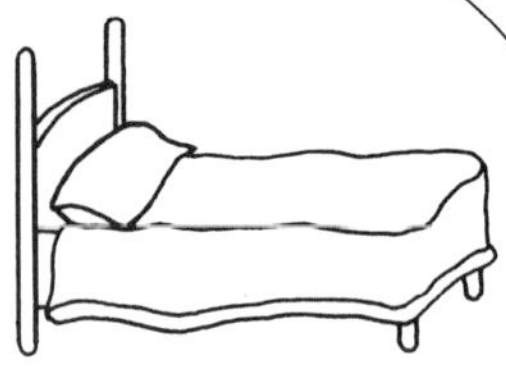
bed

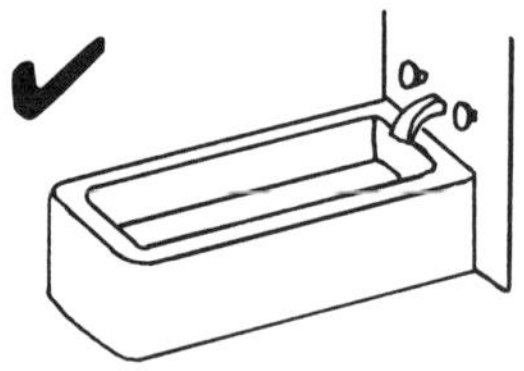
bathtub

blanket

shower

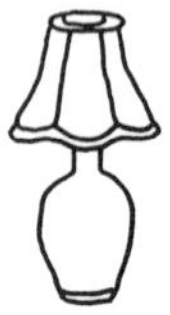
lamp

toilet

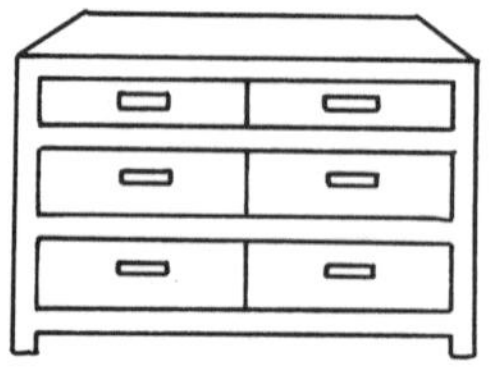
dresser/chest

closet

pillow

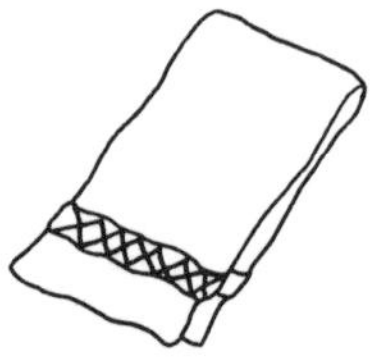
towel

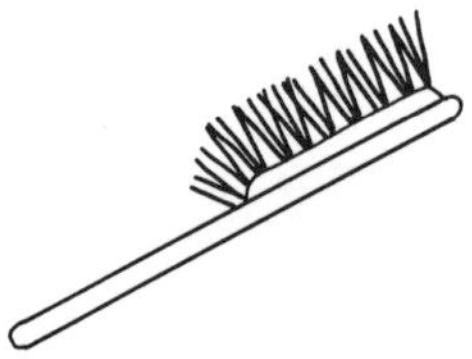
brush

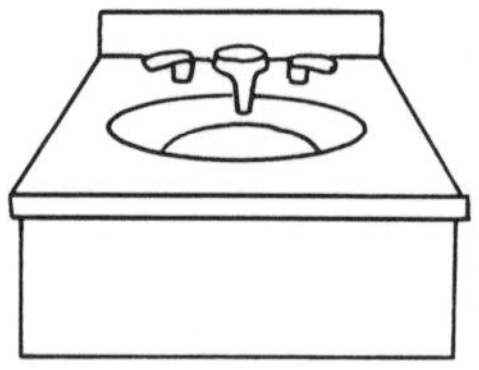
sink

toothbrush

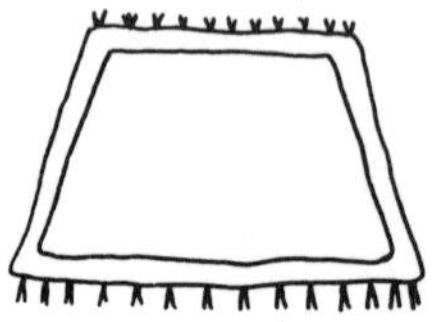
rug/carpet

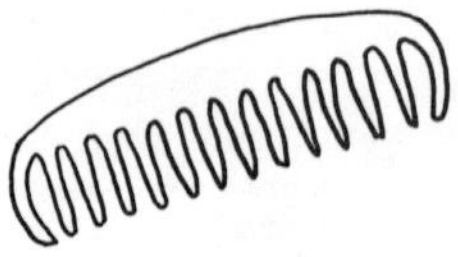
comb

soap

Draw something else for a **b**edroom or **b**athroom.	Tell about what you drew.

Balls by Boxes

Draw a **ball** . . .

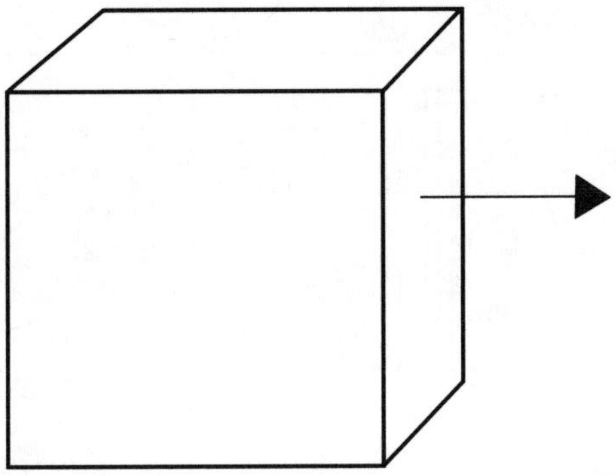

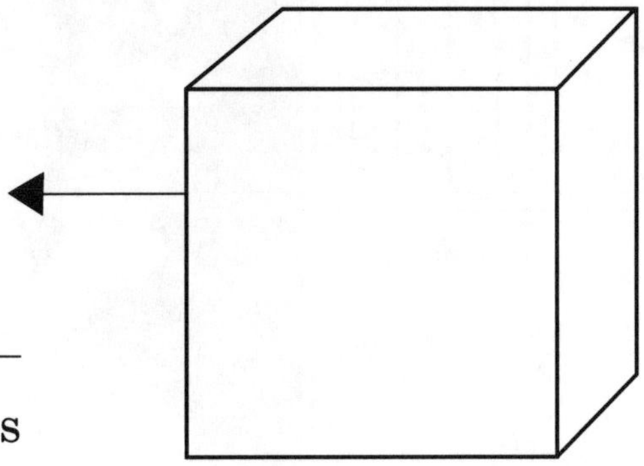

. . . **between** the **b**oxes

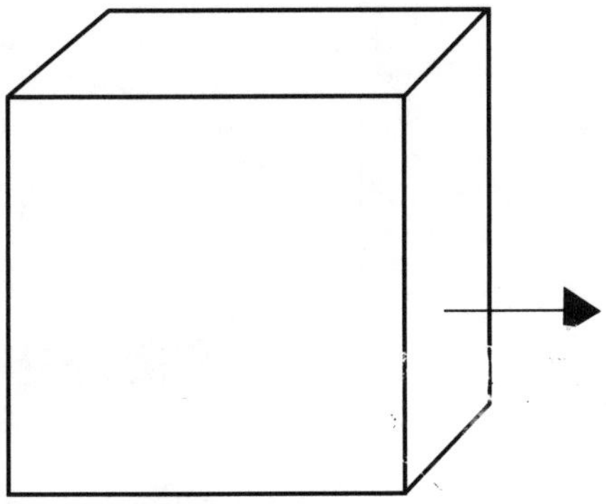

. . . **beside** the **b**ox

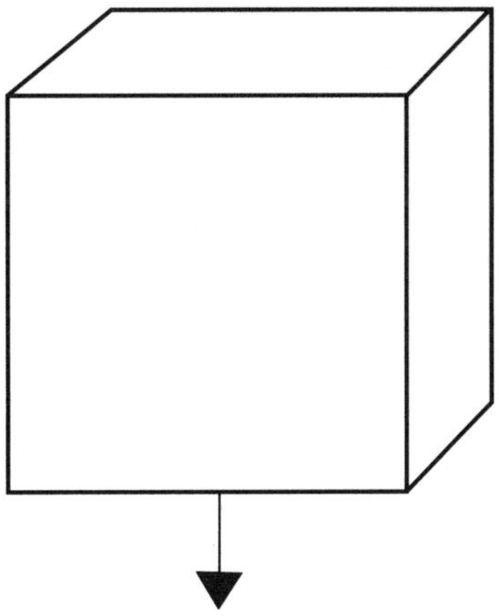

. . . **below** the **b**ox

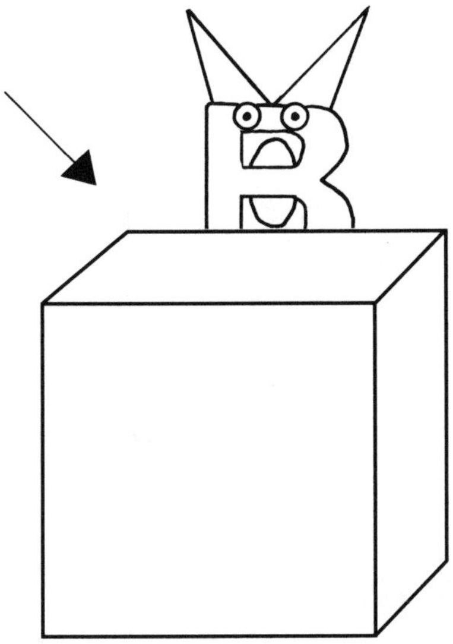

Now draw a **B** alphabet animal **behind** each **b**ox.

CAT in the CLASSROOM

Can you see the **C** *alphabet animal?*

Say the C words and color them.

Put a ✔ by these C words when you find the pictures.

___car	___cat	___cup	___clock	___cow
___castle	___chair	___clap	___computer	___circle

Cc

More C words that I found:

My C Page

cat

Draw or paste some pictures of **C** words here. Label your pictures.

Colors on the Clown

Look at the **c**olor names on your **c**rayons or **c**olored markers.

Color the shapes on the **c**lown.

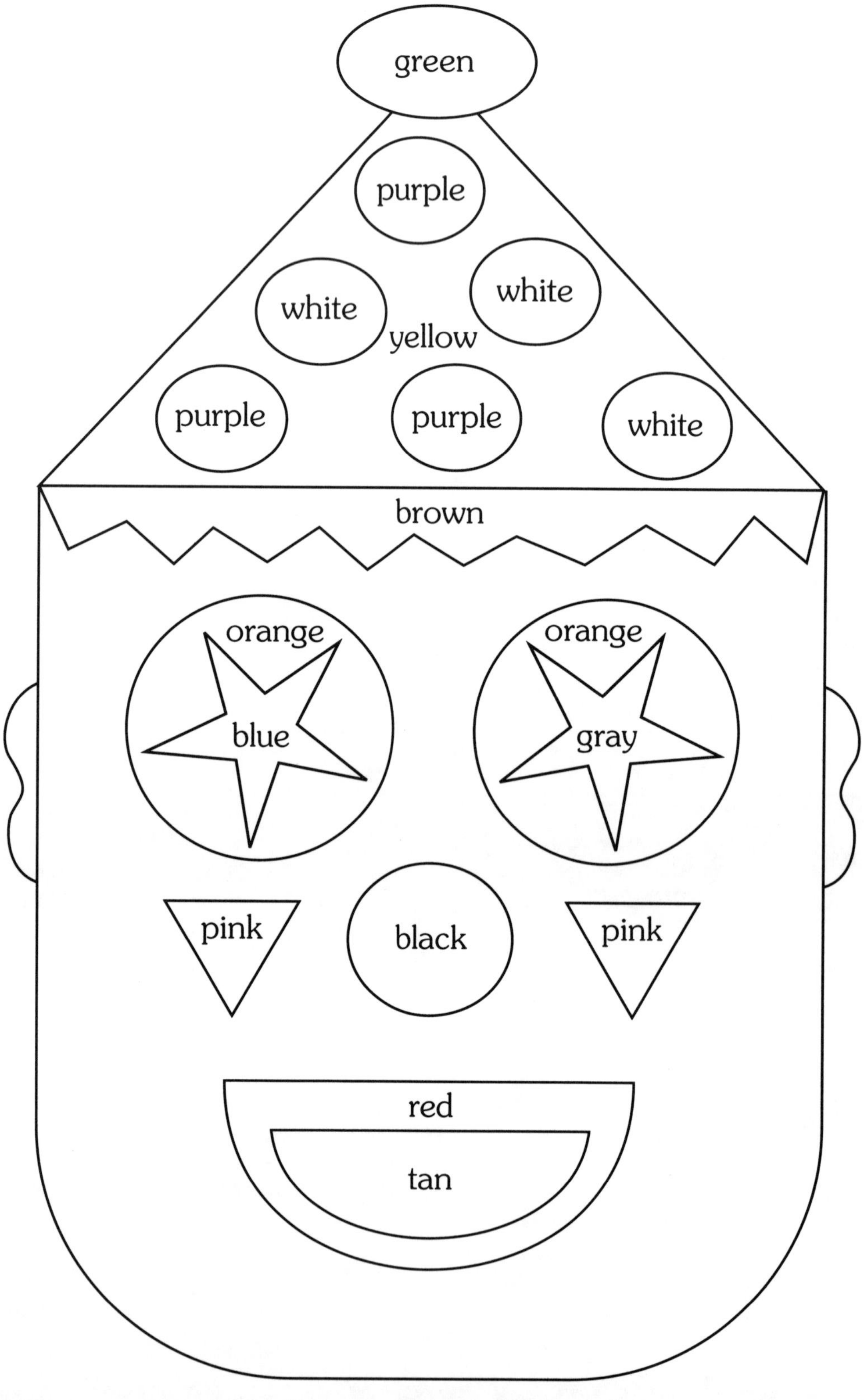

Look at the first letter of each **c**olor. Add the **c**olor names to the lists on your letter pages.

Counting

I can count from **1** to ____________.

Write more numbers.

1 2 3 ____

____

Copying the Calendar

Find a calendar for this month. Copy the name of this month on the calendar below.

Copy **1** on the correct day for this month. Copy the other numbers.

Name of this month: ______________________________

Sunday	Monday	Tuesday	Wednesday	Thursday	Friday	Saturday

Clothes

Circle the **c**lothes you are wearing today. **C**olor the **c**lothes.

necktie

cap

necklace

boots

dress

t-shirt

blouse

sweatshirt

skirt

jacket

sweater

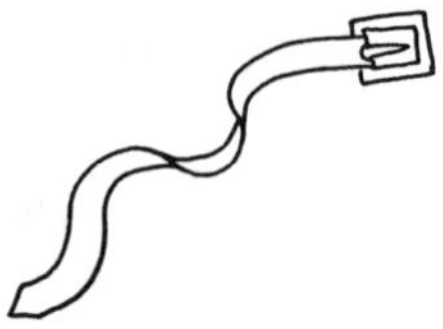
belt

socks

shoes

shorts

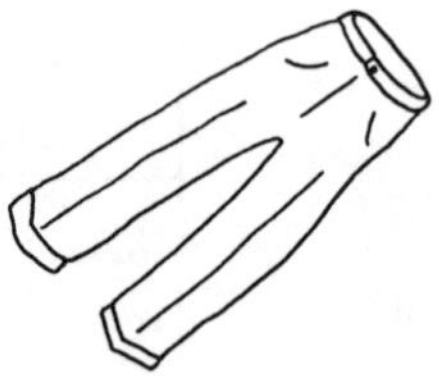
pants

Draw another piece of **c**lothing here.	Tell about what you drew.
	____________________ ____________________ ____________________

My **C**lassroom

Create a picture of your **c**lassroom. Label some of the things in it.

desk blackboard/**c**halkboard paint bookcase pen **c**lock eraser paste/glue

bulletin board **c**halk pencil notebook teacher scissors pencil sharpener

map student **c**alendar ruler wastebasket paper **c**omputer

DRAGON at DINNER

*Do you see the **D** alphabet animal?*

Say the D words and color them.

Put a ✔ by these D words when you discover the pictures.

___dog	___door	___doll	___desk	___drink
___dollar	___doctor	___dance	___dishes	___drum

Dd

More D words that I found:

My D Page

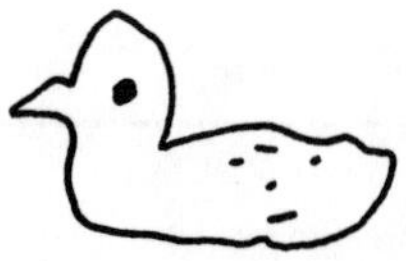

duck

Draw or paste some pictures of **D** words here. Label your pictures.

Days and **D**ates

Today's **d**ate is_____________________________________.

Circle the name of the **d**ay today.

Sunday Monday Tuesday Wednesday Thursday Friday Saturday

Draw something you **d**id today.

Different Dragons

Find the **d**ifferences in the two **d**ragons. Circle the **d**ifferences on **d**ragon #2.

Dragon #1

Dragon #2

Write about some **d**ifferences that you found.

1. ______________________________

2. ______________________________

3. ______________________________

4. ______________________________

Dot to Dot

Draw a line from **d**ot to **d**ot. What **d**id you **d**iscover? Write the word on the line below.

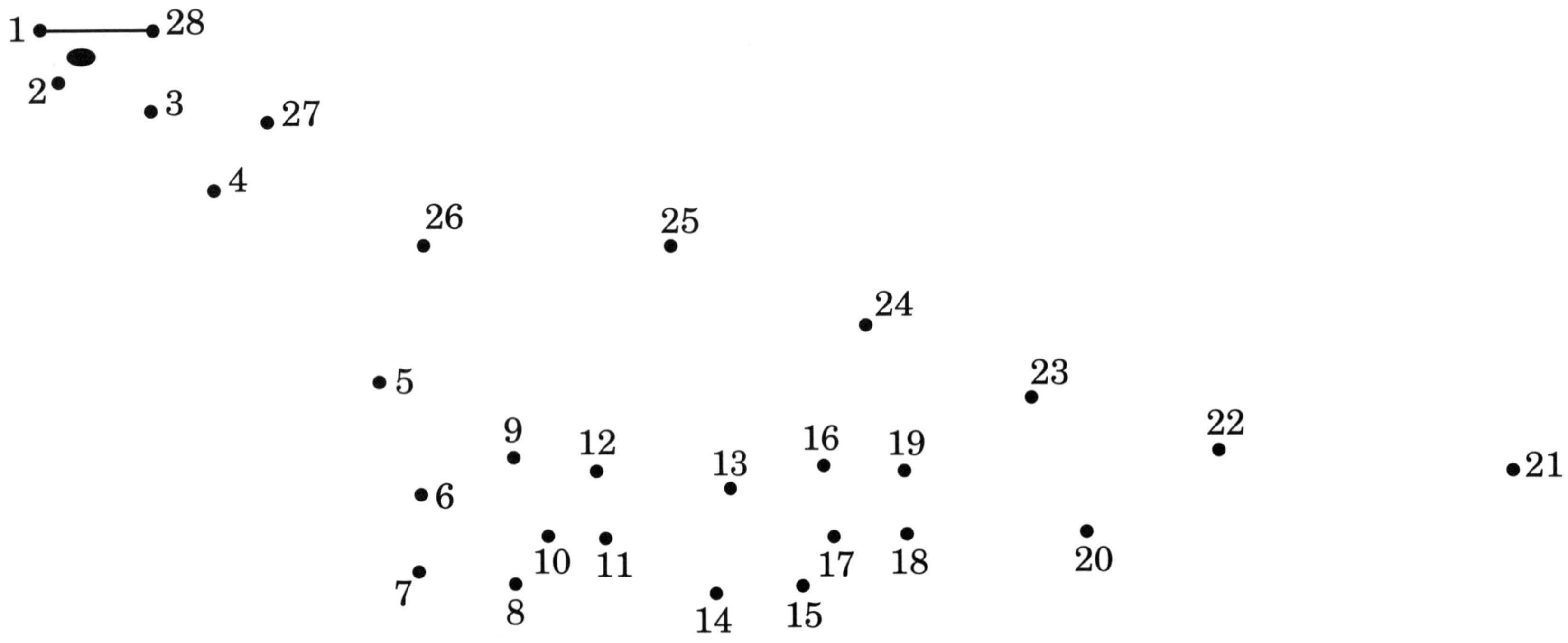

This is a ______________________________.

Draw your own **d**esign from **d**ot to **d**ot.

My Dream

Draw what you saw in a **d**ream.

Write about your **d**ream. ____________________

____

____

ELEPHANT in an ELEVATOR

*Explore for the **E** alphabet animal.*

Say the E words and color them.

Put a ✔ by these E words when you find the pictures.

___egg ___elephant ___elevator

___eraser ___exercise

Ee

More E words that I found:

______

______

______

______

______

______

______

______

______

______

______

______

______

______

______

My E Page

Draw or paste some pictures of **E** words here. Label your pictures.

Things I like to Eat

Draw some foods you **e**njoy **e**ating. Label your pictures.

Explore the Earth

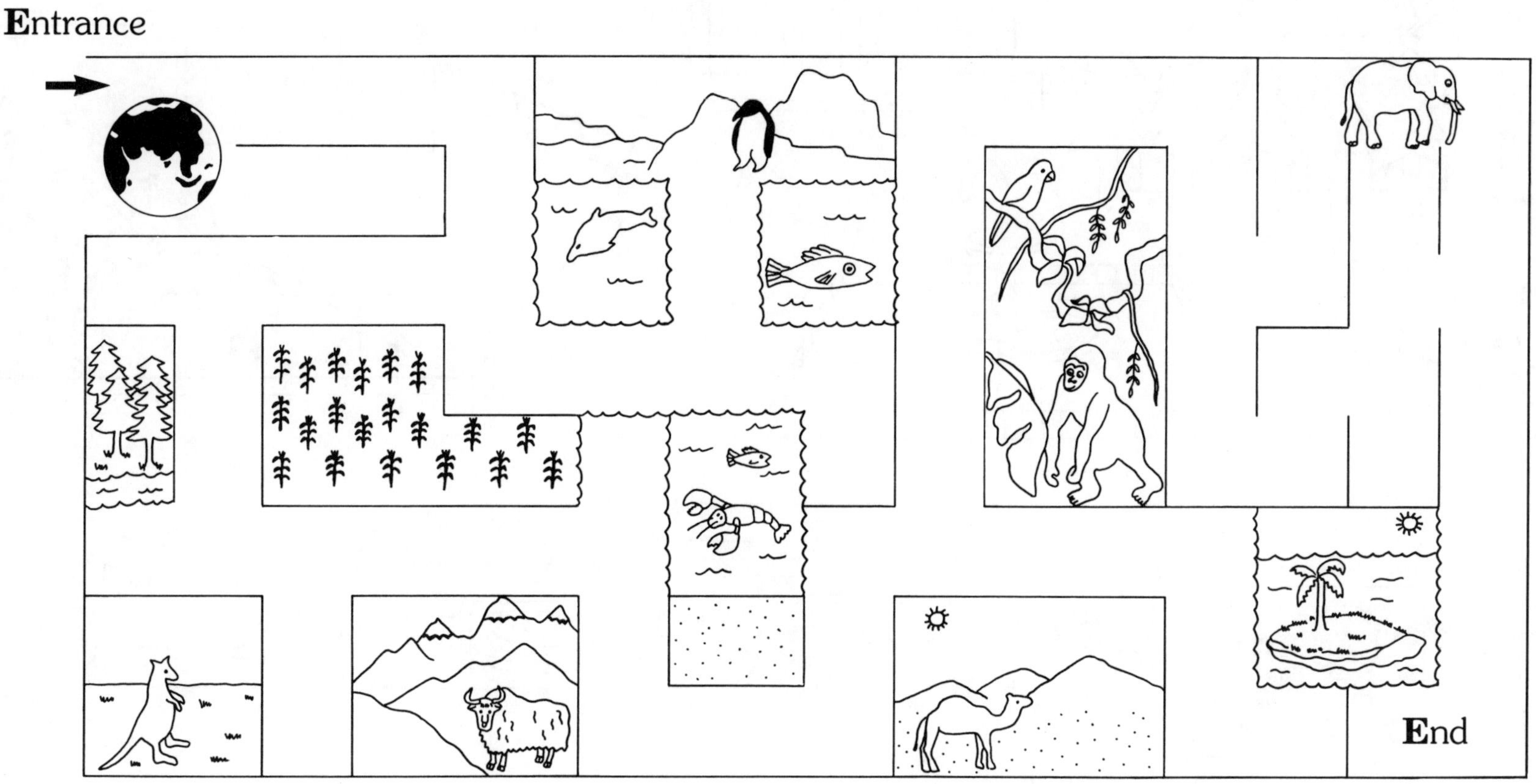

Draw your own maze. Ask someone **e**lse to **e**xplore it.

Yes No

Is the maze you drew **e**asy? _____ _____

FOXES in a FIELD

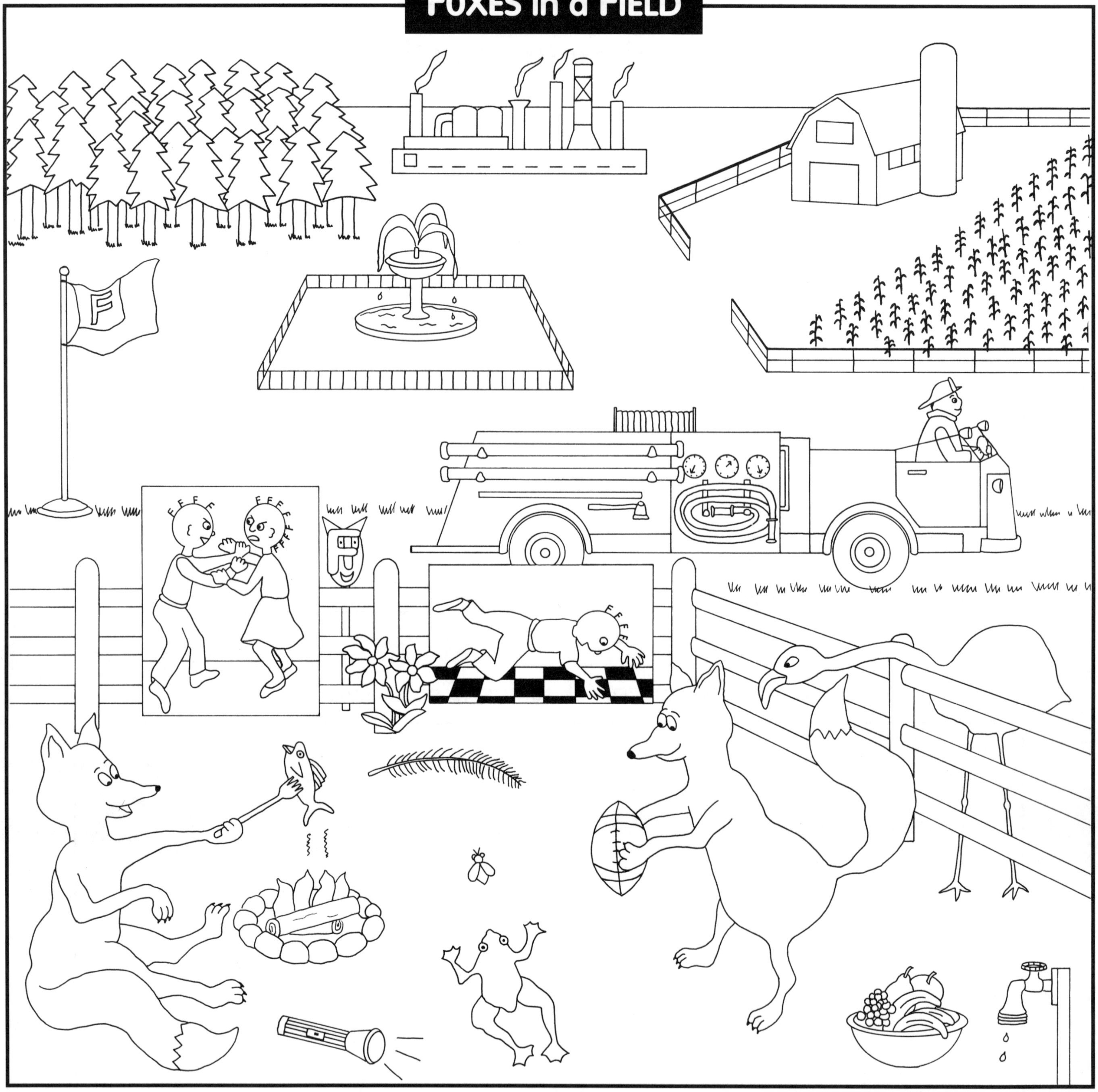

*Can you find the **F** alphabet animal?*

Say the words starting with F and color them.

Put a ✔ by these words when you find the pictures.

___farm	___fish	___fire	___fork	___fox
___flower	___flag	___frog	___football	___fruit

Ff

More words with F that I found:

My F Page

Draw or paste some pictures of words starting with **F** here. Label your pictures.

Faces

Trace the **f**eatures. Then finish the **f**ace.

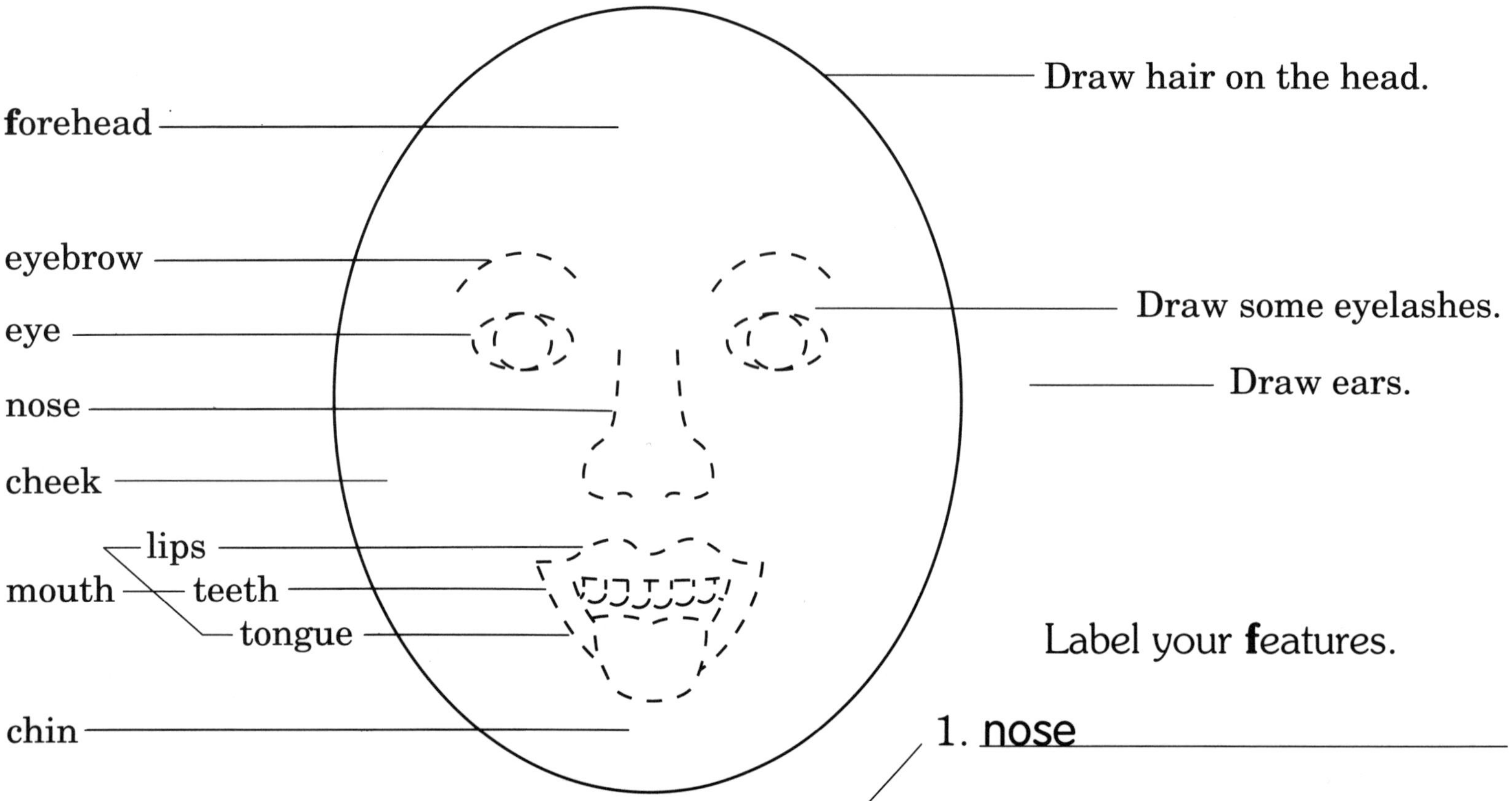

Label your **f**eatures.

1. nose
2.
3.
4.
5.
6.
7.
8.
9.
10.
11.
12.

Draw your own **f**ace.

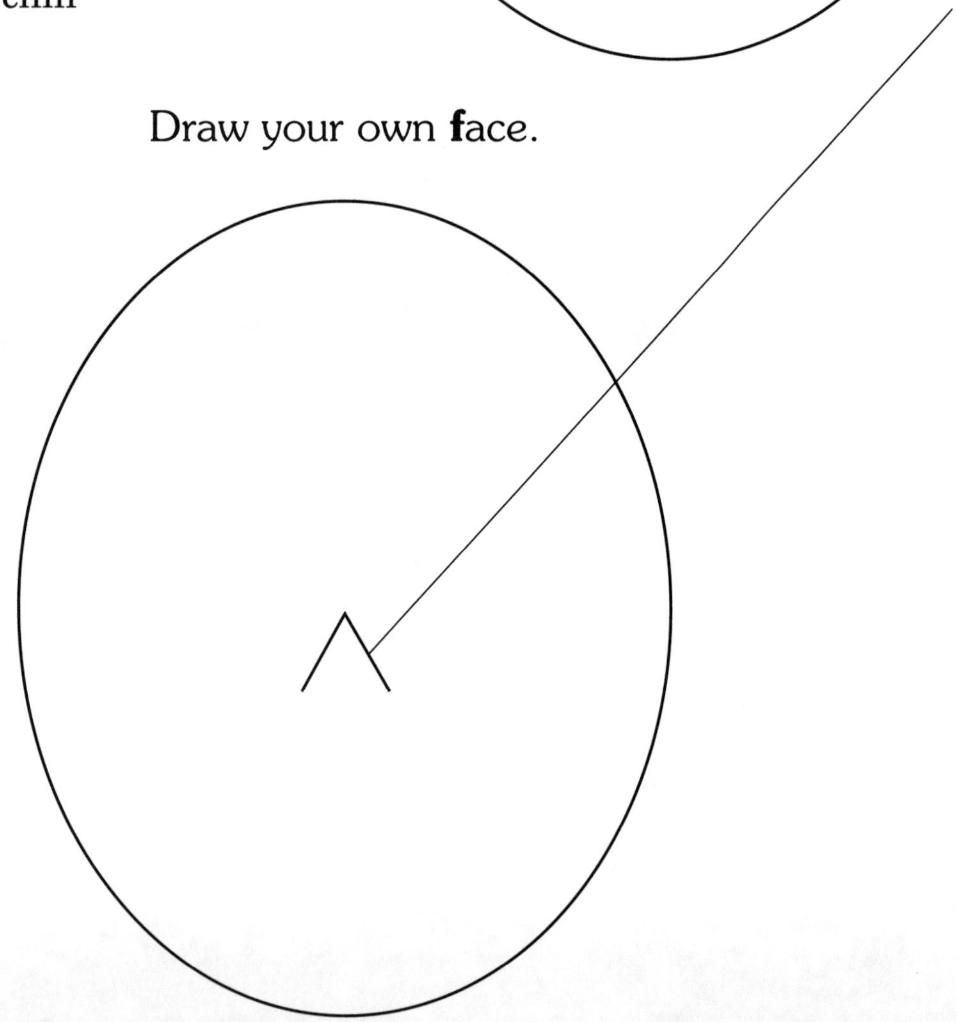

Family and Friends

Draw the faces in your family.

Put a ✔ by the family members you drew:

___ mother ___ father ___ sister ___ brother ___ aunt ___ uncle

___ grandfather ___ grandmother ___ cousin ______________________________
(another family member)

Draw a friend's face.

My friend's name is ______________________________.

Faces and Feelings

Fill in the **f**aces to show the **f**eelings.

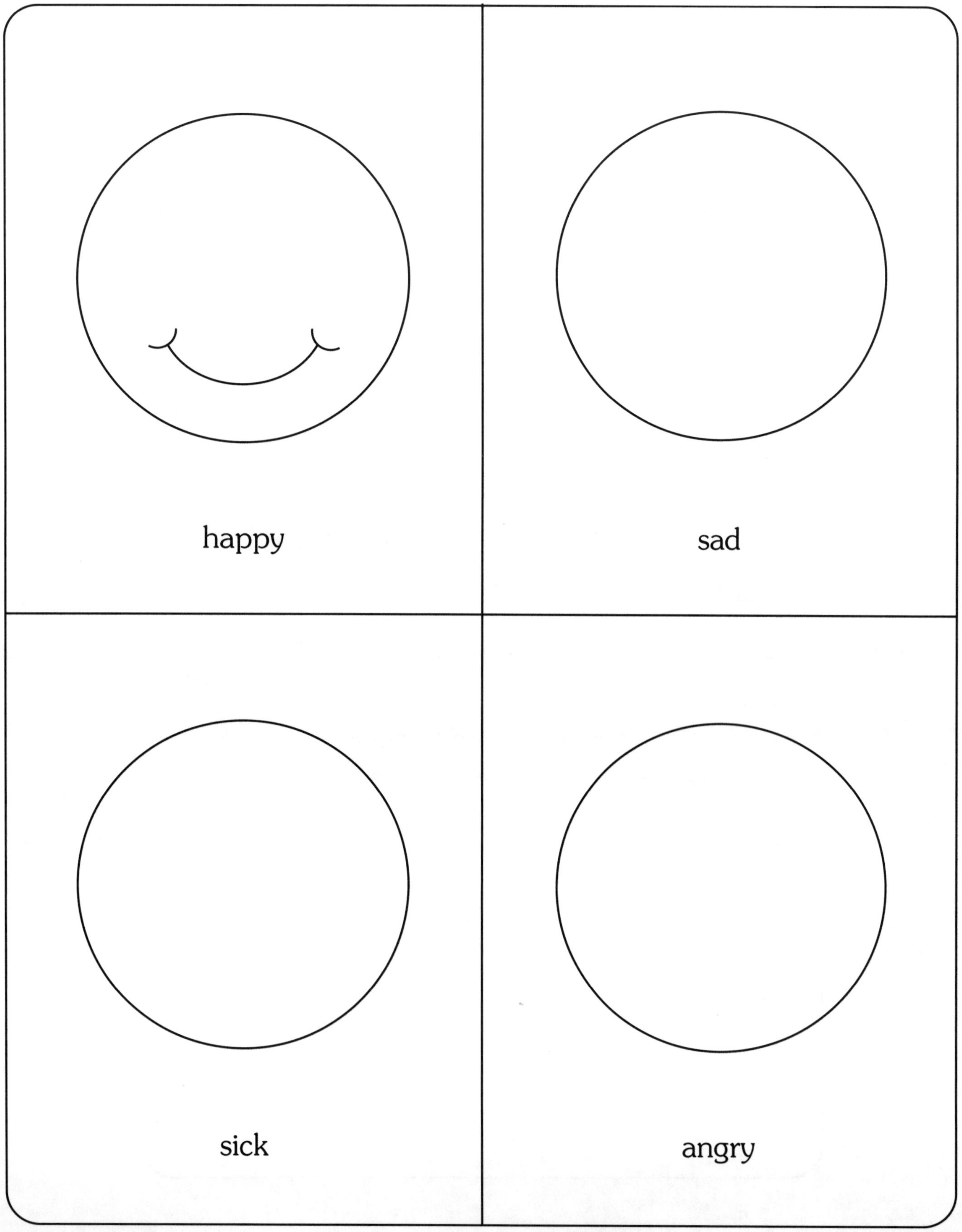

Flags

Draw the **f**lag of your country.

Find a picture of the **f**lag if you need to check the colors.

My Country's **F**lag

Design a **f**lag for yourself.

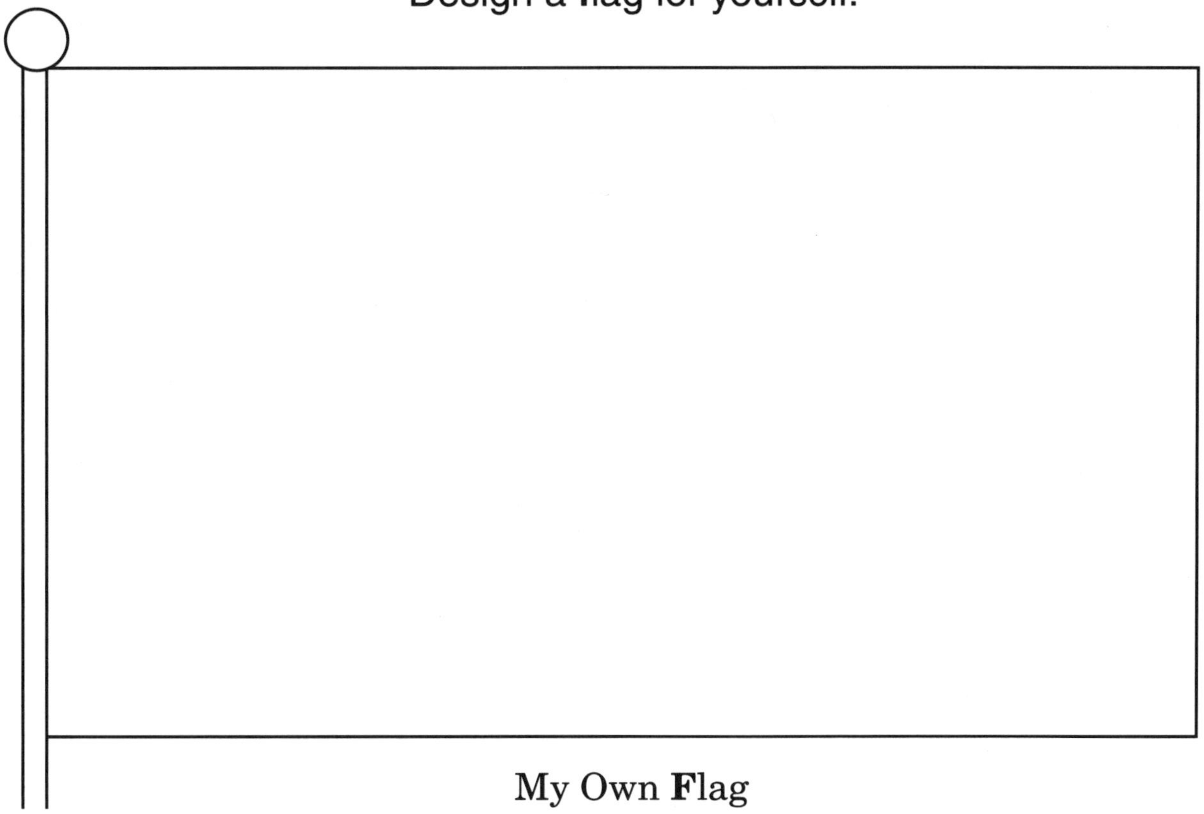

My Own **F**lag

Fruits

Circle your **f**avorite **f**ruits.

apple

avocado

bananas

cherries

grapes

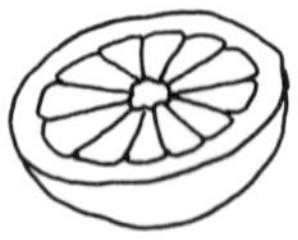
grapefruit

lemon

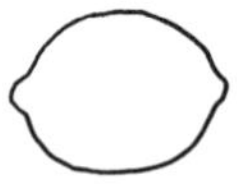
lime

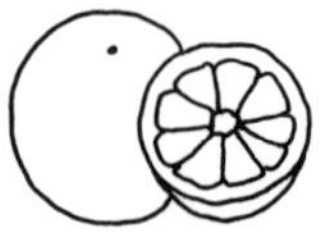
orange

peach

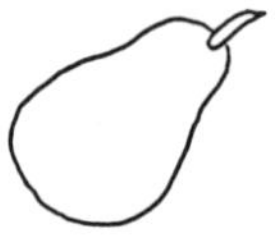
pear

pineapple

plum

raspberries

strawberries

tomato

Fill the **f**ruit bowl with some other **f**ruits.

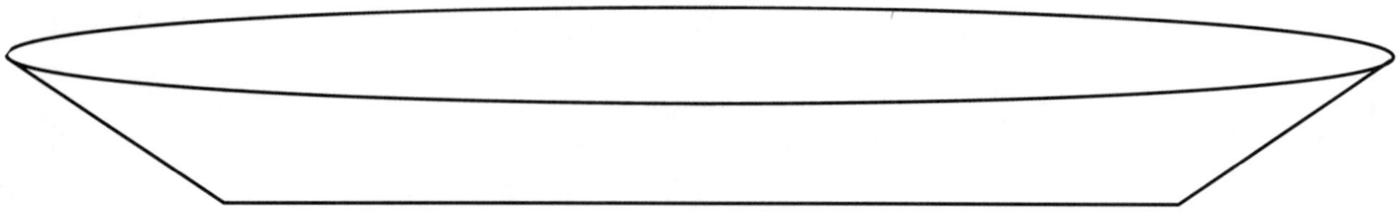

Tell about the **f**ruits that you drew. ______________________________

____

Farm **A**nimals

Find the hidden **f**arm animals in this picture.

Put a ✔ by the **f**arm animals that you **f**ind. Color them different colors.

___donkey	___pig	___horse	___goat	___chicken
___sheep	___goose	___rooster	___duck	___cow

What else did you **f**ind? ____

____

GHOST in the GARDEN

*Guess where the **G** alphabet animal is hiding.*

Say the G words and color them.

Put a ✔ by these G words when you find the pictures.

___girl	___game	___gate	___give	___garden
___giant	___giraffe	___glass	___glasses	___guitar

Gg

More G words that I found:

My G Page

gloves

Draw or paste some pictures of **G** words here. Label your pictures.

Go for the Gold!

Draw the **g**ift and the **g**old. Put numbers on the **g**ame board squares and play the **g**ame.

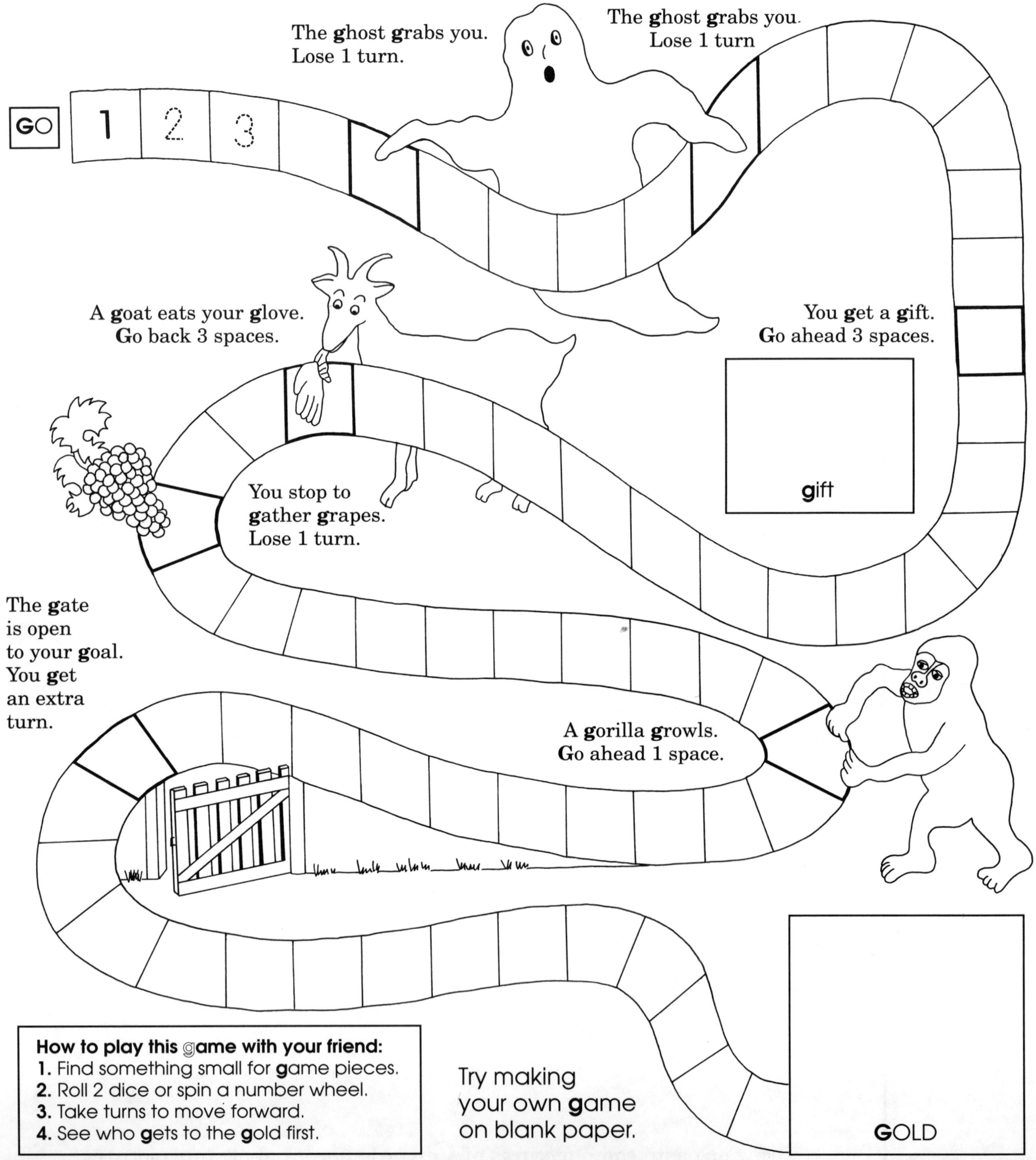

How to play this game with your friend:

1. Find something small for **g**ame pieces.
2. Roll 2 dice or spin a number wheel.
3. Take turns to move forward.
4. See who **g**ets to the **g**old first.

Try making your own **g**ame on blank paper.

Grains

Color these **g**rain foods.

bread

cereal

noodles

pancakes

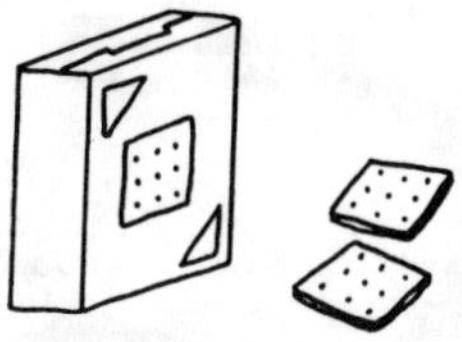

crackers

pizza

rice

sandwich

cookies

roll

Draw your favorite **g**rain foods inside this **g**rocery cart.

HIPPO HOPPING

*Have you found the **H** alphabet animal?*

Say the H words and color them.

Put a ✔ by these H words when you find the pictures.

___hat	___hole	___hose	___hill	___hug
___horn	___horse	___hammer	___helicopter	___house

Hh

More H words that I found:

My H Page

hamster

Draw or paste some pictures of **H** words **h**ere. Label your pictures.

House

Draw some furniture in this **h**ouse.
Then draw a line from the furniture to the matching word.

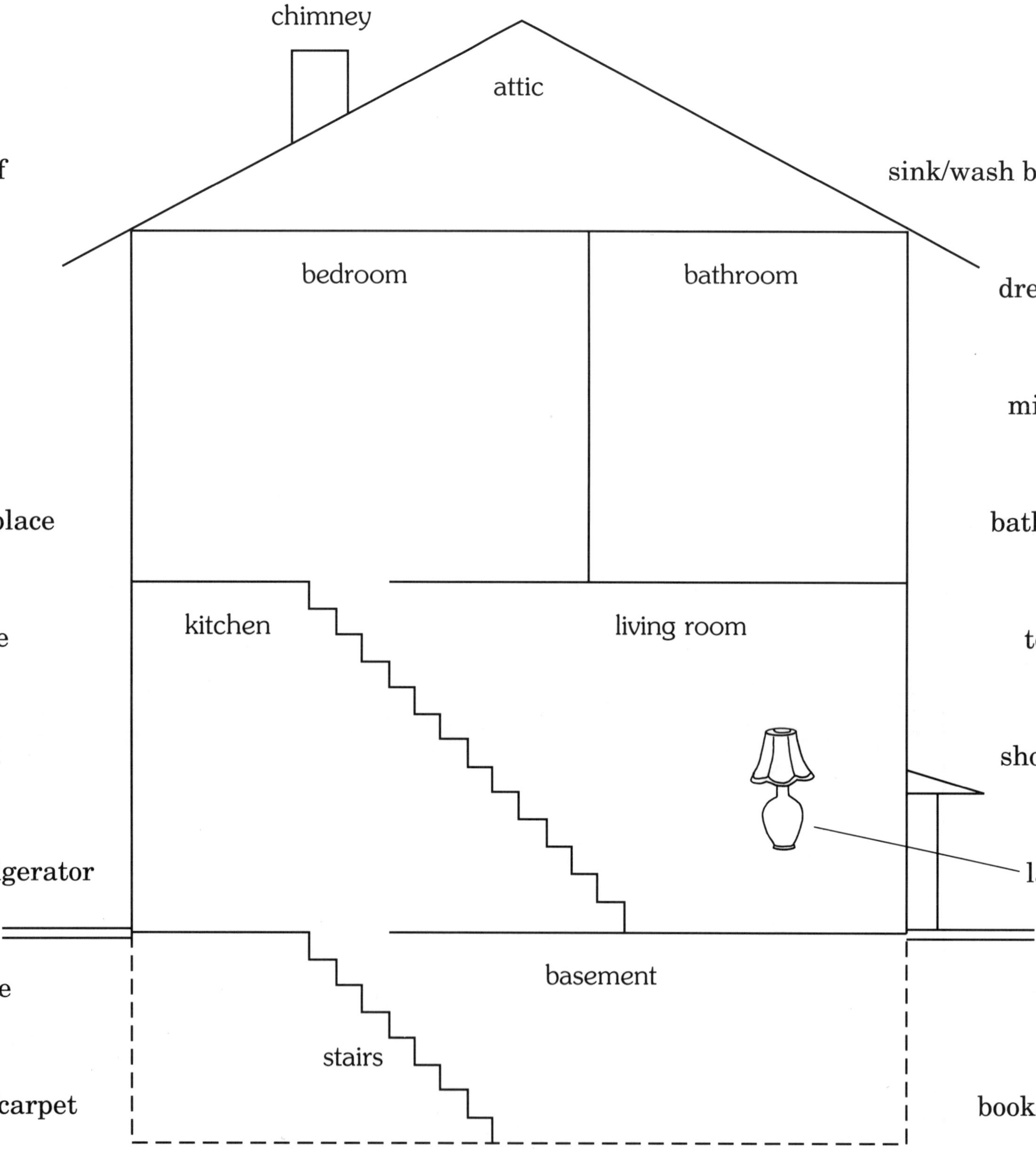

shelf
TV
bed
fireplace
table
sink
refrigerator
stove
rug/carpet

sink/wash basin
dresser
mirror
bathtub
toilet
shower
lamp
sofa
bookcase

furnace/**h**eater
washing machine
dryer
chair

My Home

Draw the place where you live. Do you live in a **h**ouse? ___Yes ___No

Tell about your **h**ome. ____

____

Holidays

What **h**olidays do you celebrate? Circle the names.
Then draw a picture of your favorite **h**oliday.

Mother's Day • Father's Day • **H**alloween • **H**anukkah • Valentine's Day • Thanksgiving

My Birthday • Easter • May Day • Children's Day • New Year's • Labor Day • Passover

Independence Day • Martin Luther King Day • Christmas • April Fool's Day • Kwanza

The name of the **h**oliday I drew is ______________________________.

How Many? 0? 1? 2?

How many **h**ands do you **h**ave? 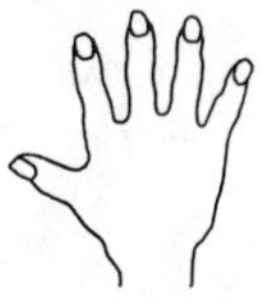 ________________

How many **h**eels do you **h**ave?  ________________

How many **h**eads do you **h**ave?  ________________

How many **h**ips do you **h**ave? 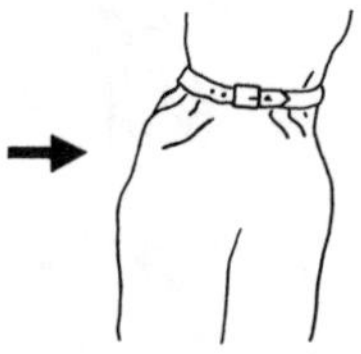 ________________

How many **h**earts do you **h**ave?  ________________

How many **h**ooves do you **h**ave? 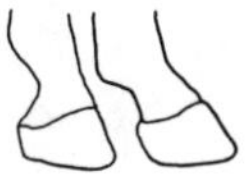 ________________

Trace your **h**and **h**ere.

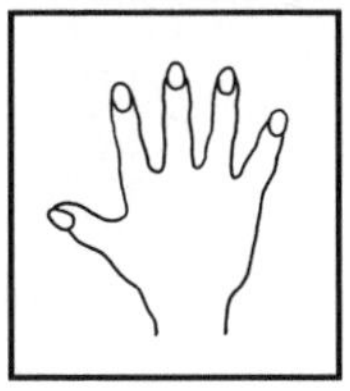

IGUANA IMAGINING

*Where is the **I** alphabet animal?*

Say the I words and color them.

Put a ✔ by these I words when you find the pictures.

___ice cream　___inch　___iguana

___ice cubes　___island

Ii

More I words that I found:

My I Page

Draw or paste some pictures of **I** words here. Label your pictures.

Imagine

What do you **i**magine **i**s **i**nside the box? Draw an **i**nteresting surprise.

Insects **in** Boxes

Draw an **insect** . . .

. . .falling **into** the box

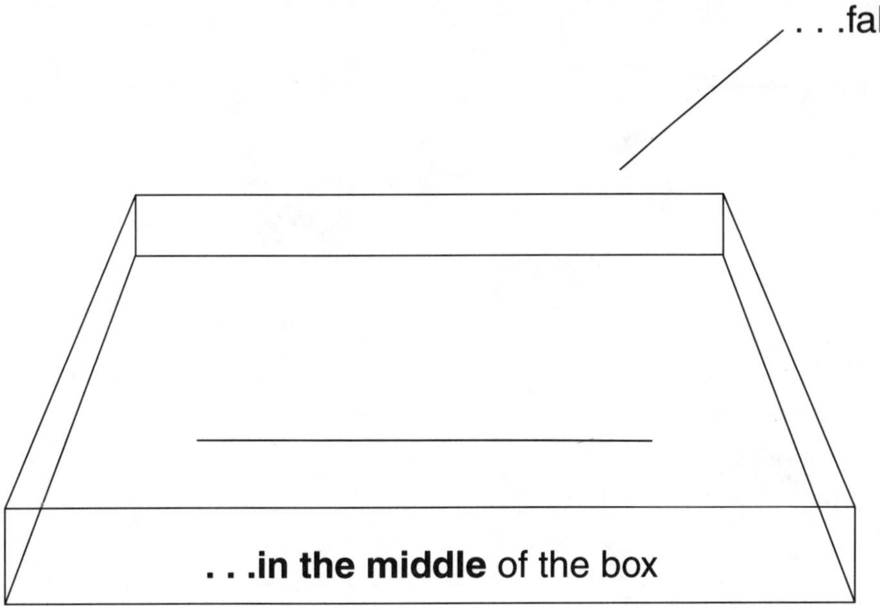

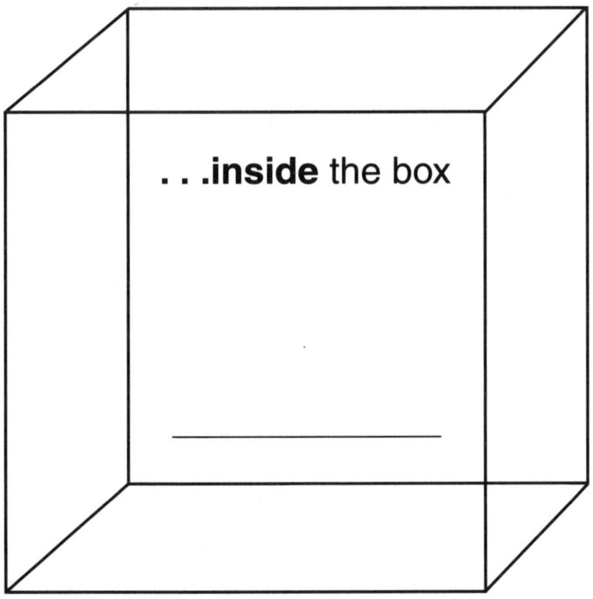

. . .**in back of** the box

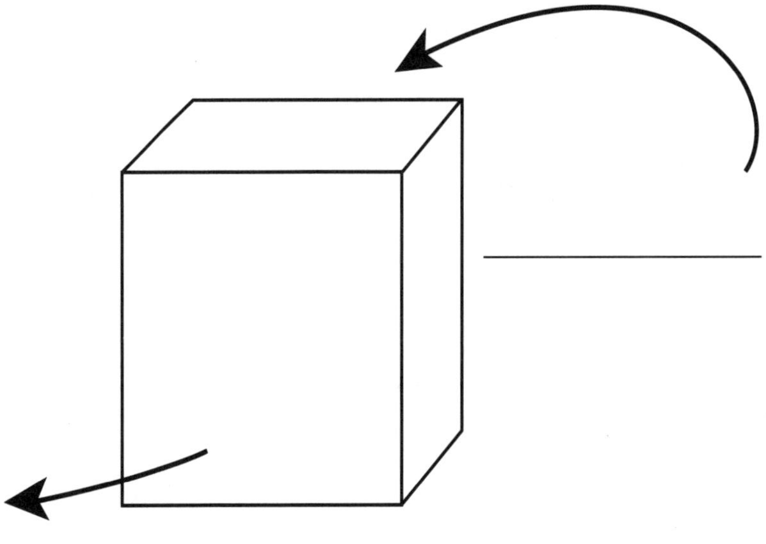

. . .**in front of** the box

JUGGLING J's

*Just where is the **J** alphabet animal?*

Say the J words and color them.

Put a ✔ by these J words when you find the pictures.

___jacket ___jeans ___juggler

___jar ___jump rope

Jj

More J words that I found:

My J Page

Draw or paste some pictures of **J** words here. Label your pictures.

Jobs

Circle the **j**obs you might like.

author

barber/hairdresser

construction worker

carpenter

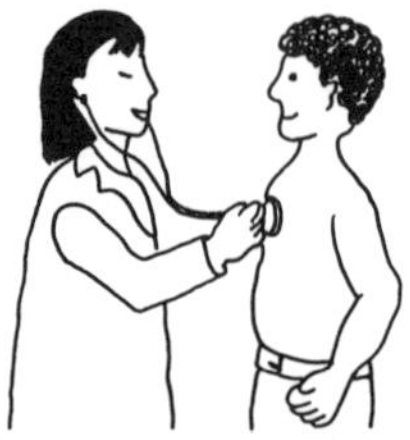

doctor

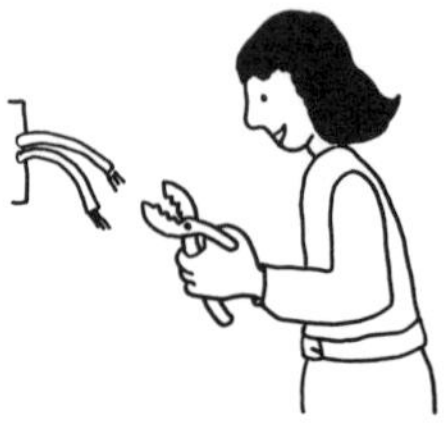

electrician

farmer

firefighter

flight attendant

football player

mail carrier

mechanic

pilot

police officer

scientist

salesperson

teacher

truck driver

TV announcer

welder

My Future Job

Draw a picture of a **j**ob you might like to have when you grow up.

Tell about the **j**ob you drew. ______________________________

____

____

KANGAROO with a KITE

*Keep looking for the **K** alphabet animal.*

Say the K words and color them.

Put a ✔ by these K words when you find the pictures.

___key

___kick

___kitten

___kite

___kangaroo

Kk

More K words that I found:

My K Page

kitten

Draw or paste some pictures of **K** words here. Label your pictures.

Kitchen Things

Circle the things that are in your **k**itchen.

bowl

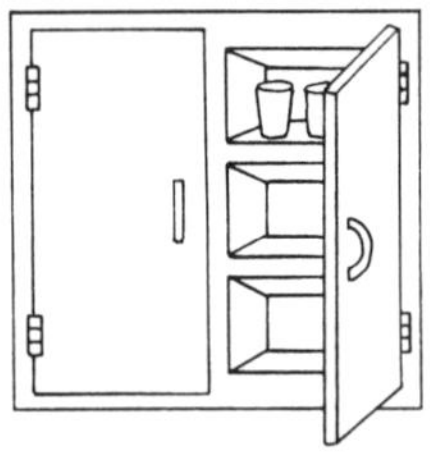
cabinet

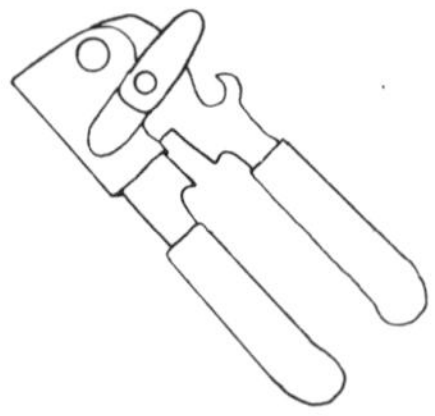
can opener

coffeepot

cup

dishes/plates

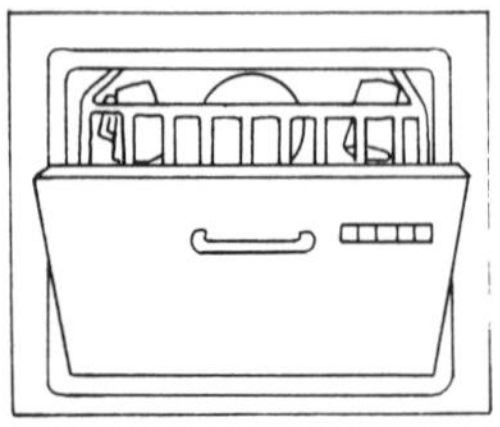
dishwasher

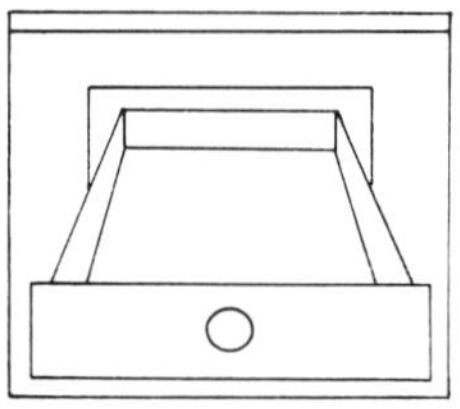
drawer

fork

glass

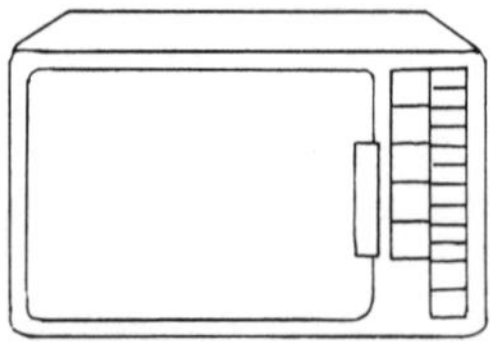
microwave oven

knife

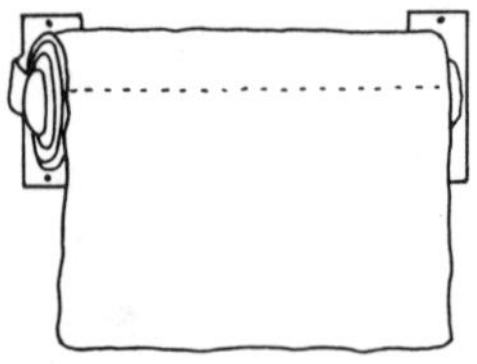
paper towels

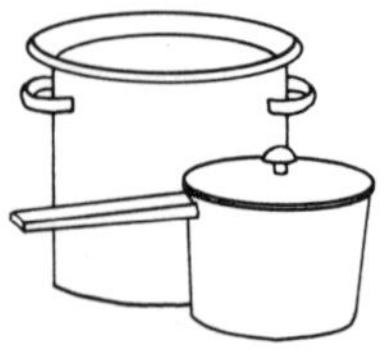
pots and pans

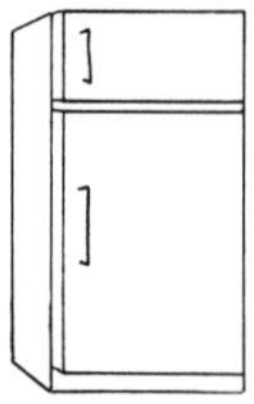
refrigerator

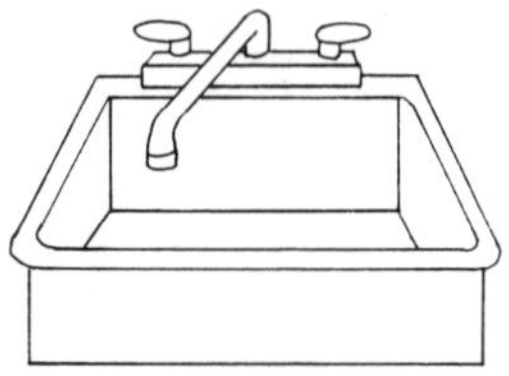
sink

spoon

stove

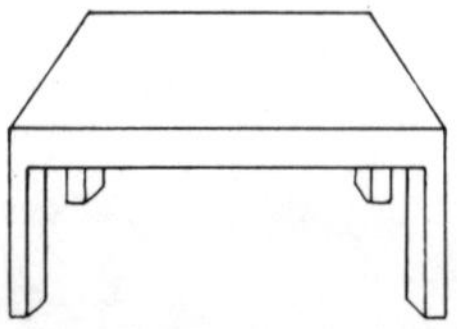
table

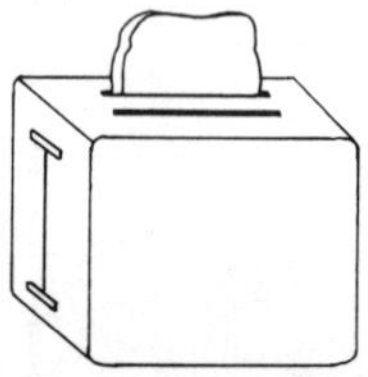
toaster

My Kitchen

Draw and label a picture of your **k**itchen.

LION by the LIVING ROOM

Look for the ***L*** *alphabet animal.*

Say the L words and color them.

Put a ✔ by these L words when you find the pictures.

___ladder	___lake	___lion	___lamp	___leaf
___lunchbox	___life jacket	___letter	___laundry	___laugh

More L words that I found:

My L Page

Draw or paste some pictures of **L** words here. **L**abel your pictures.

My Lists

Draw or list things you like and don't like.

Things I Like	Things I Don't Like
1.	1.
2.	2.
3.	3.
4.	4.

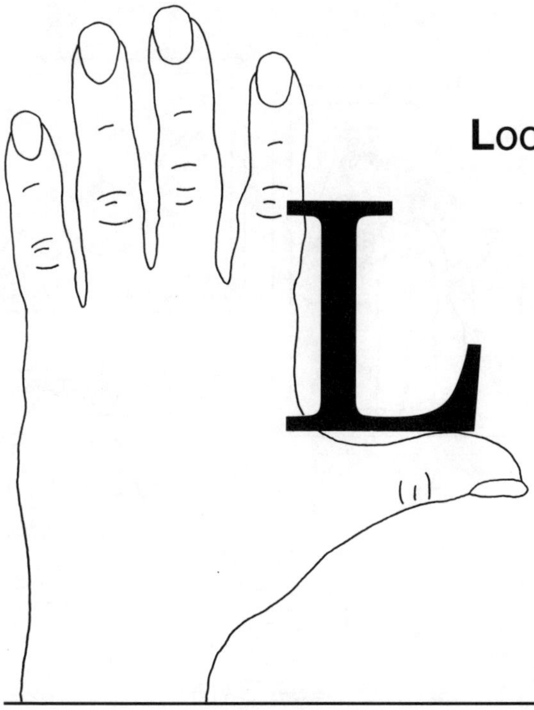

Left

Look at the back of your **l**eft hand.
Lift it in the air **l**ike this.

Trace your **l**eft hand here. Does the thumb make an **L**?

Color the **L** that your **l**eft hand makes.

MUSEUM MAGIC

*Did you miss the **M** alphabet animal?*

Say the M words and color them.

Make a ✔ by these M words when you find the pictures.

___map	___mask	___milk	___mouse	___moon
___mailbox	___magician	___mountain	___monkey	___mirror

More M words that I found:

My M Page

Draw or paste some pictures of **M** words here. Label your pictures.

Meats, Seafoods, and Dairy Foods

Circle your favorite **m**eats, seafoods, and dairy foods.

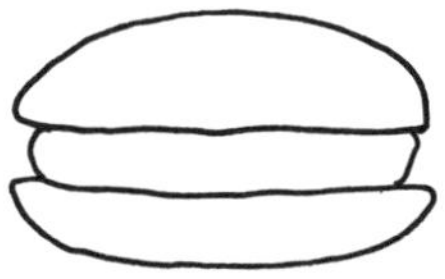

hamburger

hot dog

chicken

steak

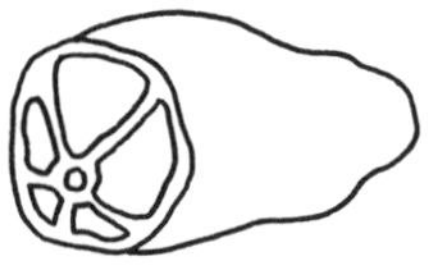

ham

lamb chops

lobster

fish

oysters

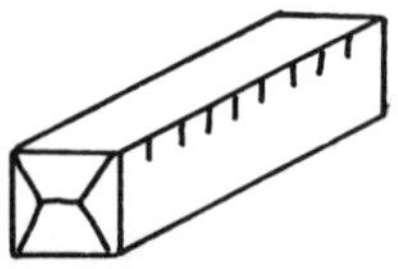

butter

milk

eggs

ice cream

yogurt

cheese

Draw another **m**eat, seafood, or dairy food here.	Tell about what you drew.
	______________________________ ______________________________ ______________________________

Measuring

Cut out the ruler on the right side of this page.
Use it to **m**easure these things.

My pencil is __________ inches long. 

My shoe is _________ inches long. 

My book is _________ inches long. 

What else can you **m**easure?
Write the names and **m**easurements here.

1. __________________________________ ____________ inches long

2. __________________________________ ____________ inches long

Months of the Year

Circle your birthday **m**onth.

January	February	**M**arch	April
May	June	July	August
September	October	November	December

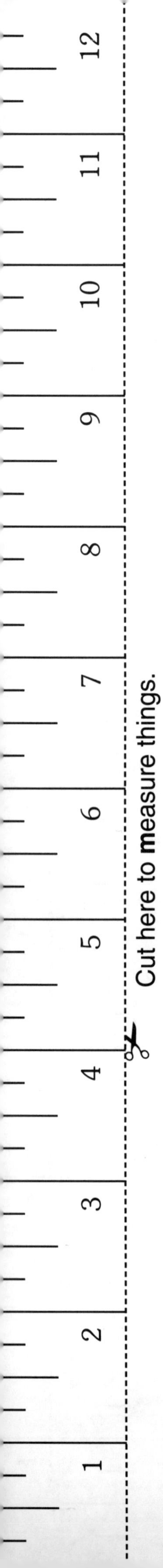

My Mystery Map

Make a secret treasure **m**ap.

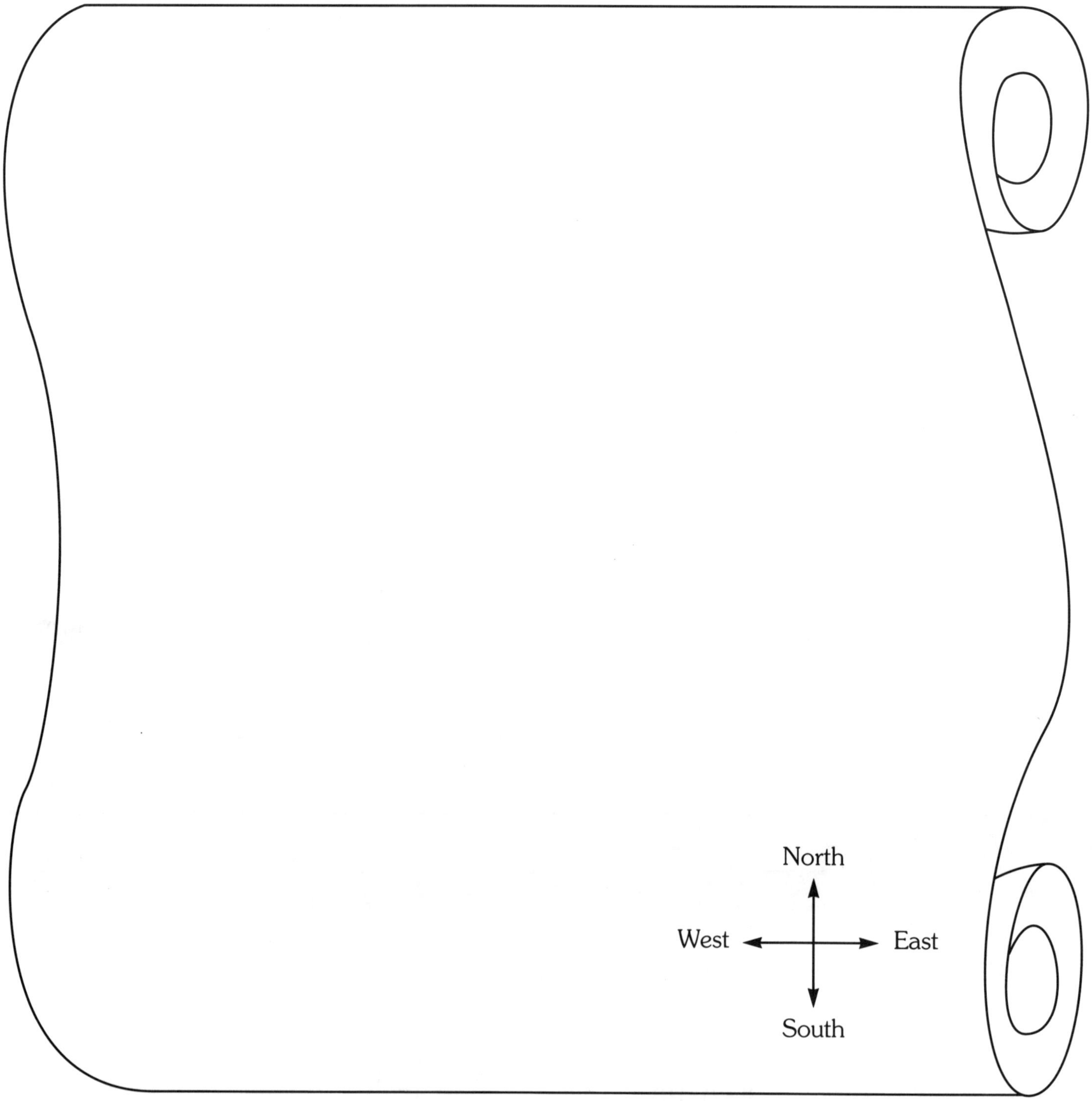

Tell what the pictures on your **m**ap **m**ean:

________ **m**eans a road

________ **m**eans ________

________ **m**eans ________

Matching Money

Make lines to **m**atch equal amounts of **m**oney.

1 quarter

1 dollar (100 cents)

1 dime

1 nickel

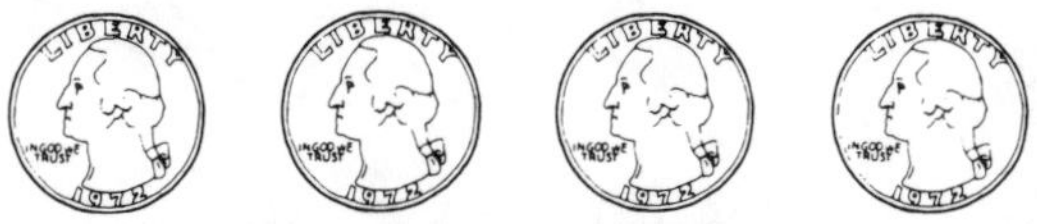

4 quarters

10 dimes

2 dimes + 1 nickel

5 pennies

2 nickels

Make a **m**agic **m**oney picture.

Put this paper over a  coin. Rub it with a pencil or crayon to **m**ake **m**agic.

NURSE near a NEST

*Now can you find the **N** alphabet animal?*

Say the N words and color them.

Put a ✔ by these N words when you notice the pictures.

___net ___nest ___number ___nurse ___nail

___necklace ___notebook ___nightgown ___newspaper ___napkin

Nn

More N words that I found:

My N Page

Draw or paste some pictures of **N** words here. Label your pictures.

No ⃠ Not

What do the signs mean? Write the words below the signs.

No

dogs

Now make your own sign and tell what it means.

1. **N**o buses	5. **N**o dogs
2. **N**o parking	6. **N**o turning
3. **N**o motorcycles	7. **N**o bicycles
4. **N**o smoking	8. **N**o trucks

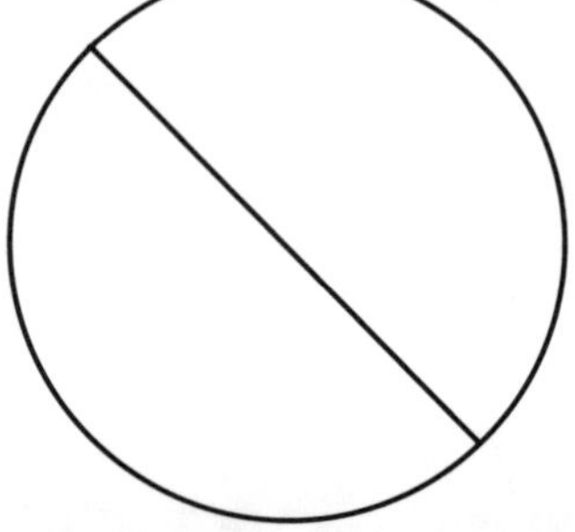

Next **N**umber

Write the **n**ext **n**umbers in these rows.

0, 1, 2, 3, 4, ______
next?

0, 2, 4, 6, 8, ______
next?

Now write your own **n**umber pattern.

0 ______ ______ ______ ______
next? **n**ext? **n**ext? **n**ext?

Next Picture

NnNnNnNnNnNnNnNnNnNnNnNnNnNnNnNnNnNnNnNnNnNnNnNnNnNnNnNnN

Look at this picture.

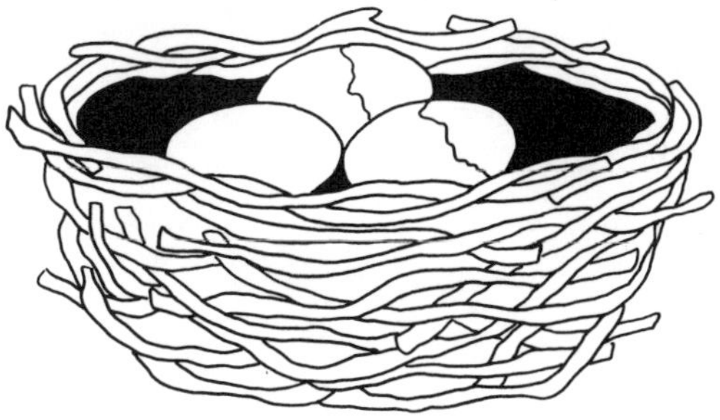

Draw what comes **n**ext.

Tell about the pictures. ______

NnNnNnNnNnNnNnNnNnNnNnNnNnNnNnNnNnNnNnNnNnNnNnNnNnNnNnNnN

OWL on an OSTRICH

*Where is the **O** alphabet animal?*

Say the O words and color them.

Put a ✔ by these O words when you observe the pictures.

___oven ___open ___onion

___octopus ___ocean

More O words that I found:

Oo

My O Page

Draw **or** paste some pictures **of** **O** words here. Label your pictures.

Orchestra

Circle the instruments that you usually see in an **o**rchestra.

accordion

cello

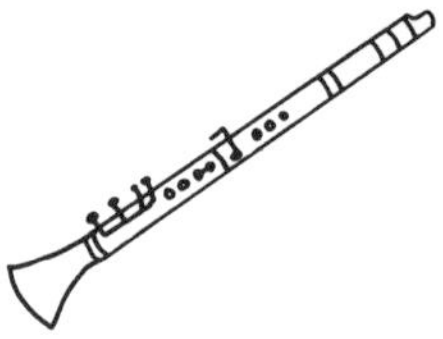
clarinet

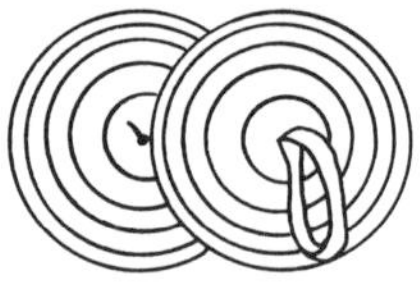
cymbals

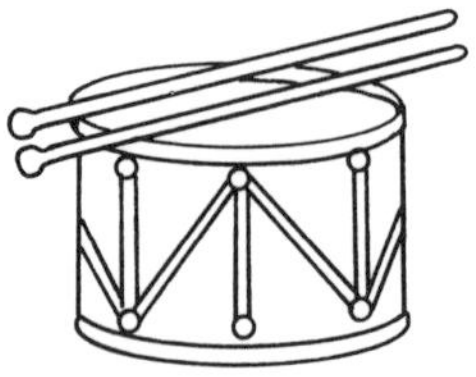
drum

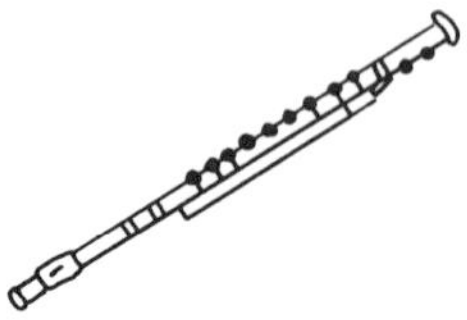
flute

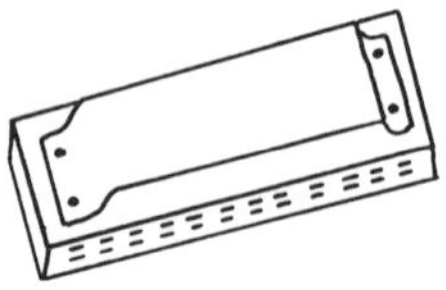
harmonica

harp

maracas

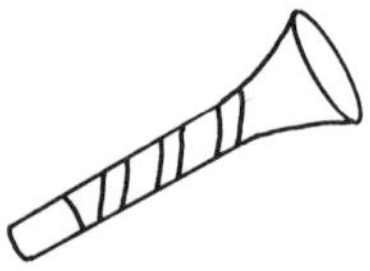
party horn

tambourine

trumpet

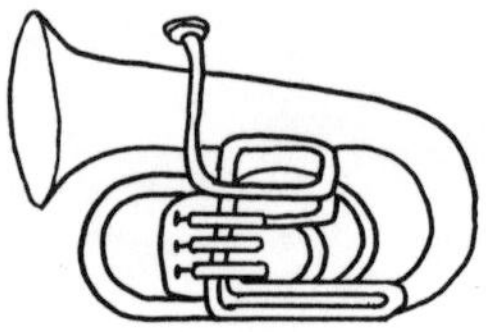
tuba

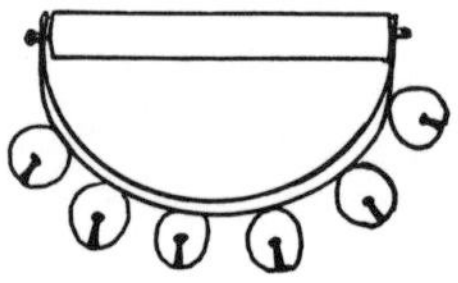
sleigh bells

violin

whistle

Draw another **o**rchestra instrument here.	Tell about the instrument you drew.
	______________________ ______________________ ______________________

Oranges **on** Boxes

Draw an **o**range . . .

. . . **on** the box ________________

____

. . . **over** the box

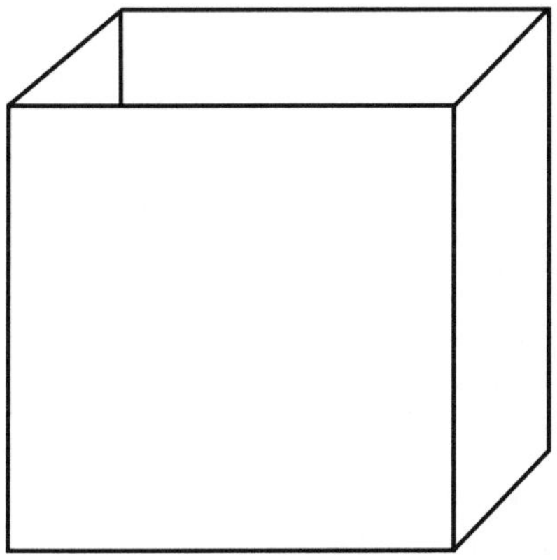

____

. . . **outside** the box

. . . rolling **off** the box

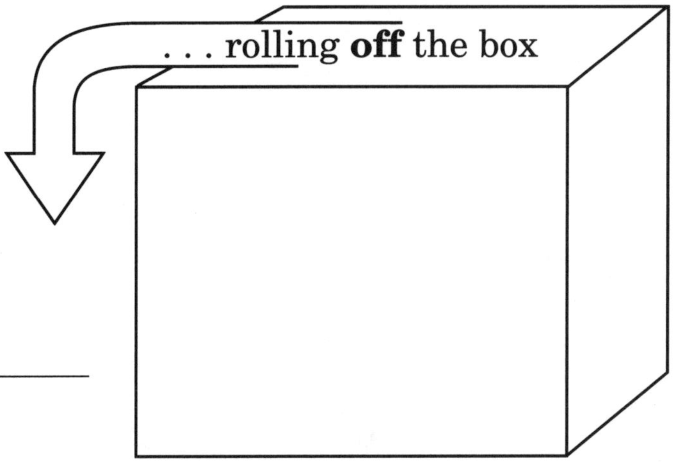

____

PICNIC in the PARK

*Can you see the **P** alphabet animal **p**eeking out?*

Say the P words and color them.

Put a ✔ by these P words when you find the pictures.

___pencil	___piano	___picnic	___panda	___pig
___pillow	___puppet	___paintbrush	___parachute	___pizza

Pp

More P words that I found:

My P Page

Draw or **p**aste some **p**ictures of **P** words here. Label your **p**ictures.

Plants and their **P**laces

Match the **p**lants ....with the **p**laces where they grow.

cactus 

pine forests 

flowers and bushes 

fields of corn 

seaweed 

tropical vines 

mountains 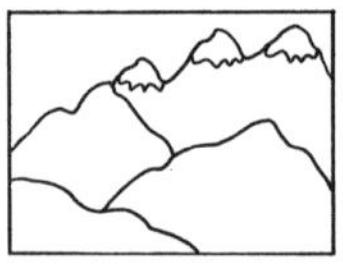

jungle 

ocean 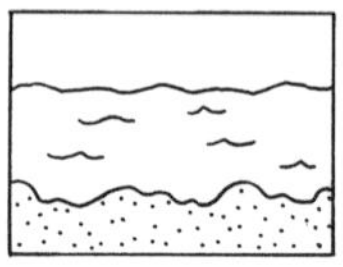

desert 

yard 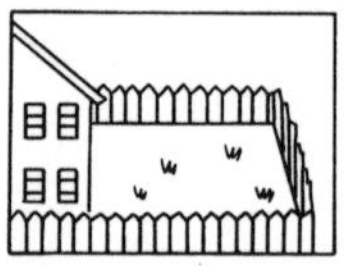

farm 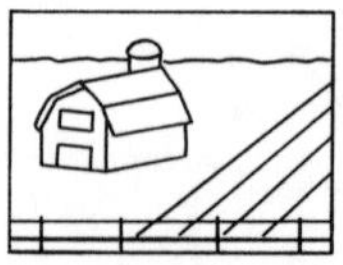

Draw and label another **p**lant.

Tell about the **p**lace
where your **p**lant grows.

____

____

____

____

Pets?

Circle the animals that are good house **p**ets.

cat

gorilla

horse

lobster

hippopotamus

angelfish

goat

dog

jellyfish

bee

bird

rat

lion

Draw a **p**icture of your favorite **p**et.

THE QUEEN'S QUILT

Quiz yourself. Where is the ***Q*** *alphabet animal?*

Say the Q words and color them.

Put a ✔ by these Q words when you find the pictures.

___quilt ___queen ___quart

___quarter ___question mark

Qq

More Q words that I found:

My Q Page

quarter

Draw or paste some pictures of **Q** words here. Label your pictures.

Question Words

Make a **q**uiz with these **q**uestion words.
Think of some **q**uestions and write them on the lines.
Ask a friend to write the answers.

Question:

Where does a queen live ?

Answer: in a castle.

Question:

What ______________________________?

Answer: ______________________________

Question:

When ______________________________?

Answer: ______________________________

Question:

Who ______________________________?

Answer: ______________________________

The Queen's Castle

Draw a castle where a **q**ueen might live.

Who else lives in the castle? ______________________________

____

ROBOT at the RACE

Remember to look for the ***R*** *alphabet animal.*

Say the R words and color them.

Put a ✔ by these R words when you find the pictures.

___rabbit	___river	___race	___rain	___read
___ring	___road	___rope	___refrigerator	___radio

Rr

More R words that I found:

My R Page

Draw or paste some pictures of **R** words here. Label your pictures.

Ride and **R**oll

Circle your favorite ways to **r**ide.

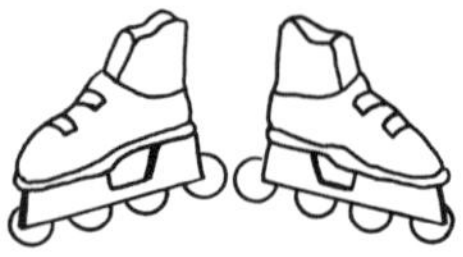
on **r**oller skates

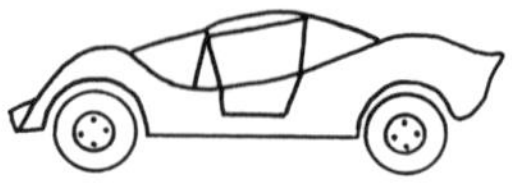
in a **r**ace car

in a truck

in an airplane

on a **r**oller coaster

on a bicycle

on a horse

on a boat

on a motorcycle

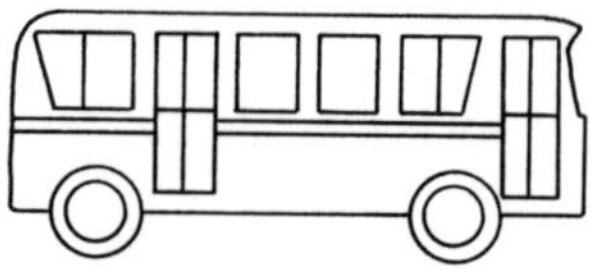
on a bus

on a skateboard

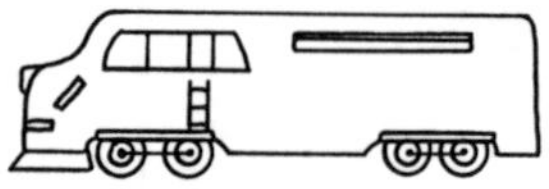
on a train

Draw a picture of something you like to **r**ide.

I like to **r**ide ____.

The Robot Story

Once there was a  named **R**obert. He had a 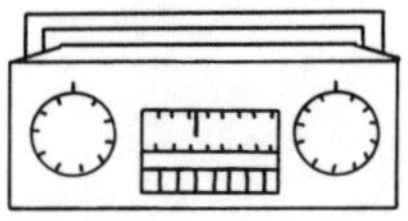 inside him.

He had 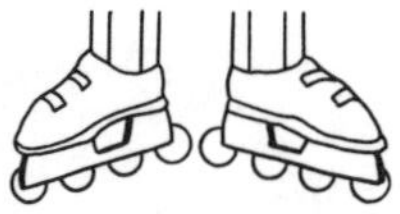 for feet. He could  and **r**emember lots of things,

but he could not go out in the  or he would get **r**usty. One day **R**obert's friend,

the , found **R**obert's **r**emote control and . . .

Draw what happened next.

Tell the **r**est of the story. ______________________________

____

____

SEAL with a SWORD

*Search for the **S** alphabet animal.*

Say the S words and color them.

Put a ✔ by these S words when you see the pictures.

___sun	___socks	___star	___snake	___spoon
___ship	___shell	___shelf	___scissors	___street

Ss

More S words that I found:

My S Page

Draw or paste some pictures of **S** words here. Label your pictures.

(S) Person

What is **S** person doing? Write the words below the pictures.

smelling

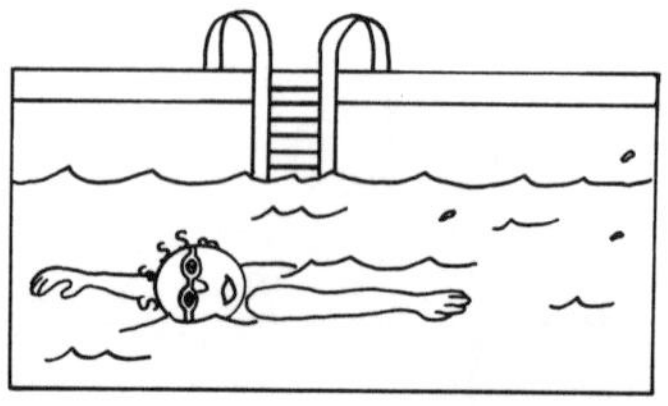

___sleeping
___singing
___sewing

✔smelling
___swimming
___smiling

___sweeping
___standing
___sitting

Shapes

triangle

diamond

Draw **s**omething with **s**everal **s**hapes in it.

star

circle

square

rectangle

heart

oval

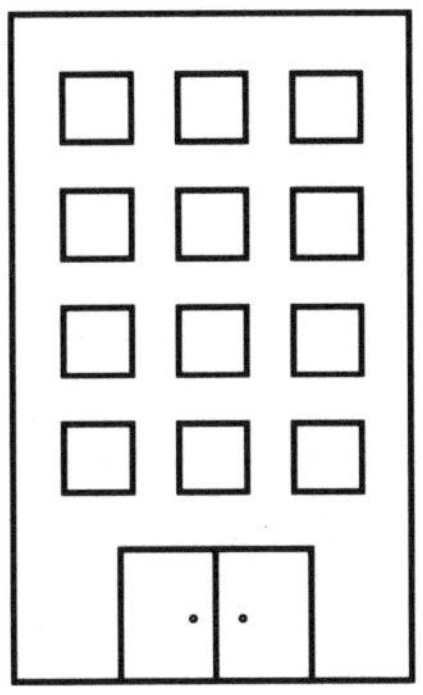

Seasons

Show each **s**eason. Put different colors on the tree branches.

Winter: gray icicles

Spring: pink flowers

Fall: orange and yellow leaves

Summer: green leaves

My favorite **s**eason is ______________________________.

Sizes

small   medium   large   extra large

Draw a different **s**ize pair of **s**hoes on each person.

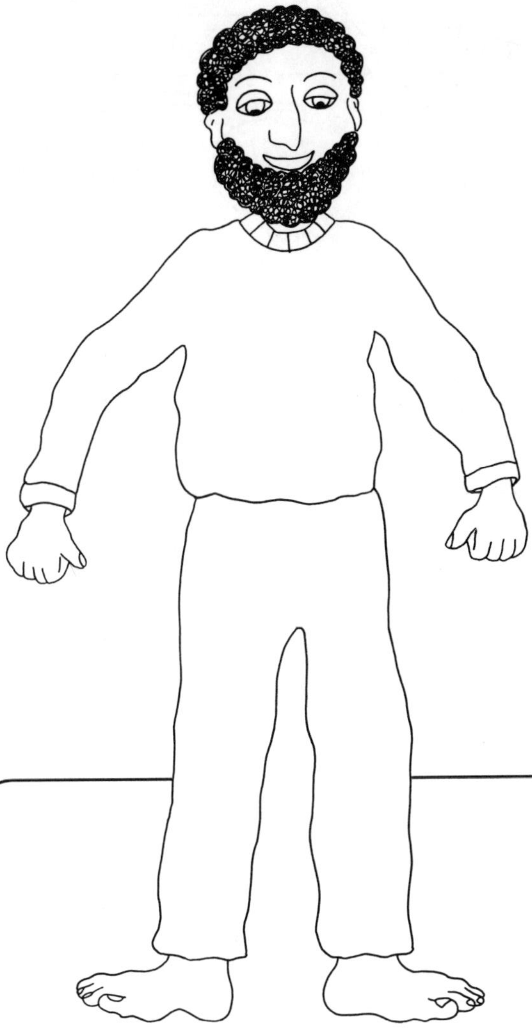

extra large **s**hoes

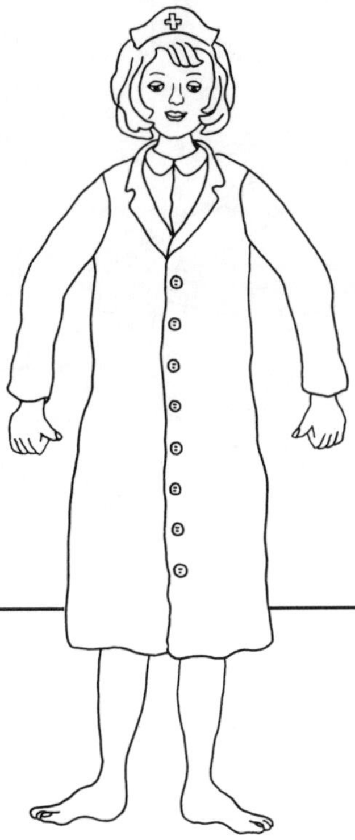

large **s**hoes

medium-**s**ized **s**hoes

small **s**hoes

A TIGER for TEA

*Try to find the **T** alphabet animal.*

Say the T words and color them.

Put a ✔ by these T words when you find the pictures.

___table	___turtle	___tiger	___train	___truck
___television	___telephone	___teddy bear	___thermometer	___throw

Tt

More T words that I found:

______

______

______

______

______

______

______

______

______

______

______

______

______

______

______

My T Page

Draw or paste some pictures of **T** words here. Label your pictures.

Train Travel

Trace the train tracks.
Try to get to town.

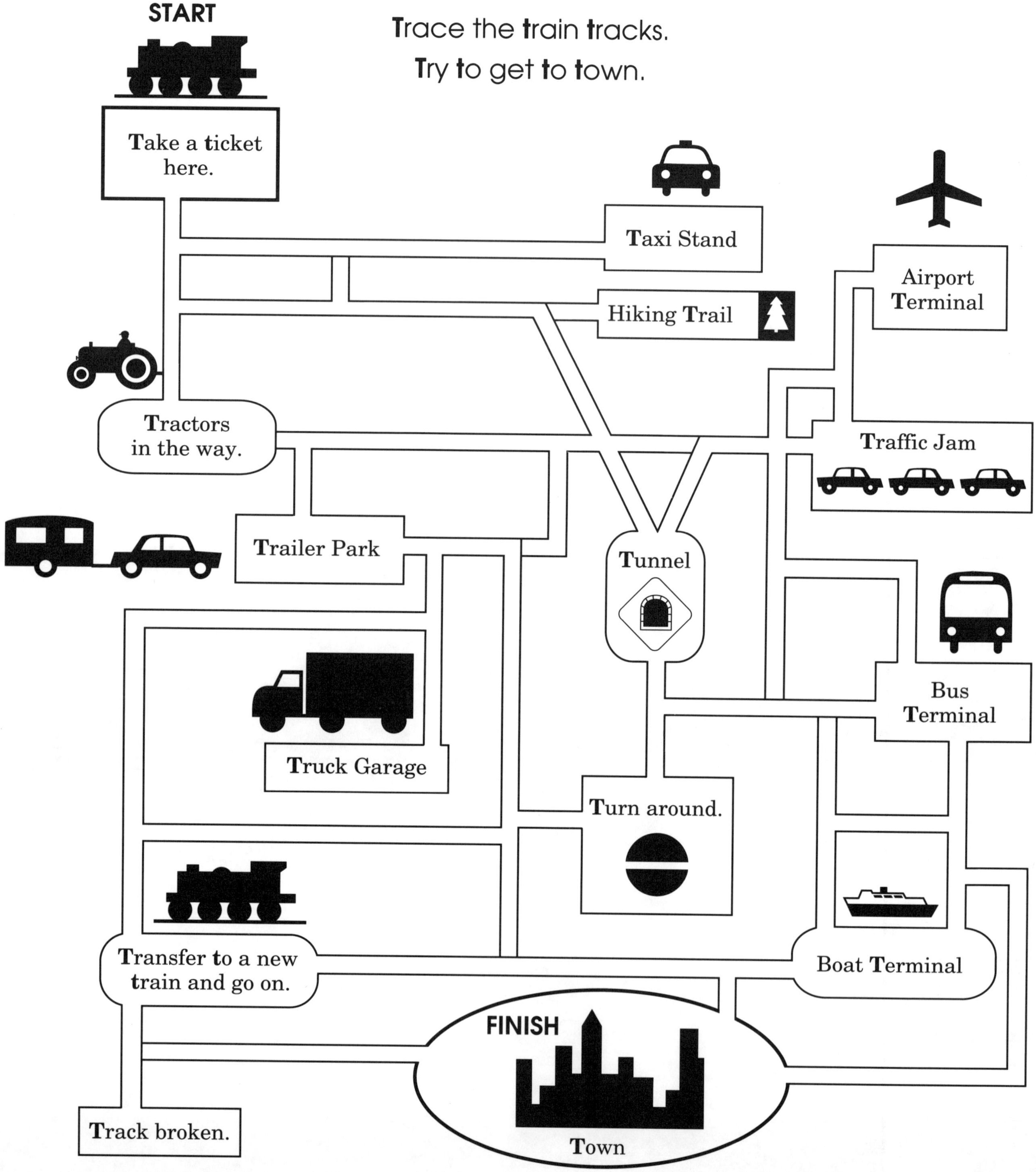

My Favorite TV Program

What is **t**he name of **t**he **T**V program? ______________________________

Tell about **t**his **T**V program. ______________________________

____

____

UPSIDE DOWN under an UMBRELLA

*Look up at the picture. Find the **U** alphabet animal.*

Say the U words and color them.

Put a ✔ by these U words when you find the pictures.

___umbrella

___umpire

___usher

___unicorn

___underwear

Uu

More U words that I found:

My U Page

Draw or paste some pictures of **U** words here. Label your pictures.

Useful Things

Circle the things that you know how to **u**se.

fork

spoon

knife

paintbrush

hammer

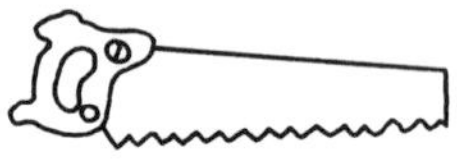
saw

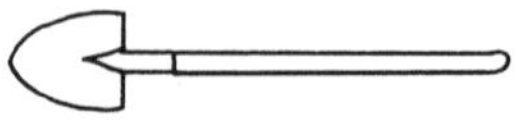
shovel

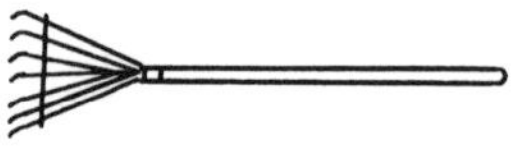
rake

screwdriver

needle

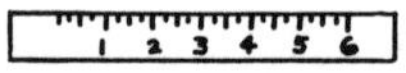

ruler

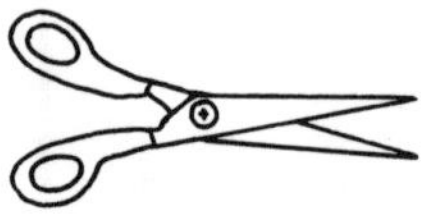
scissors

Draw something else you know how to **u**se.

I know how to **u**se a ______________________________.

Bugs **under** Boxes

Draw an **u**gly

. . .

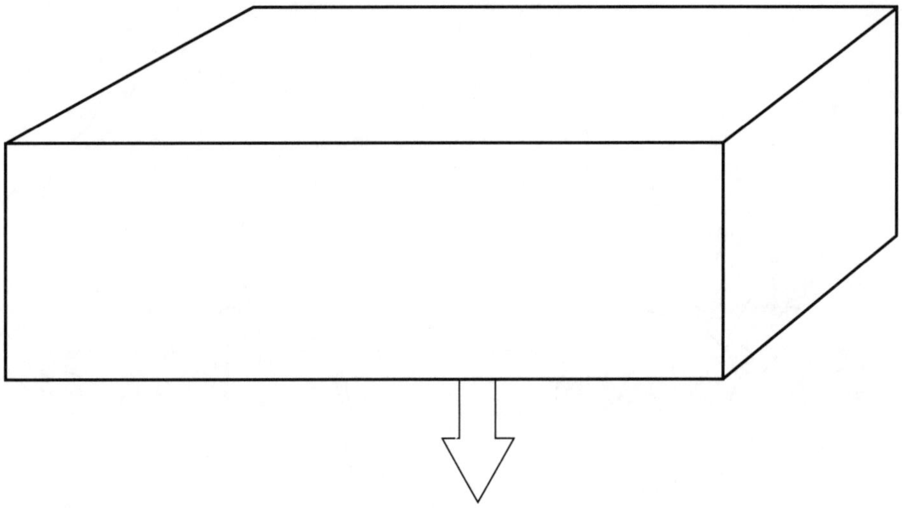

. . . **under** the box ____________________

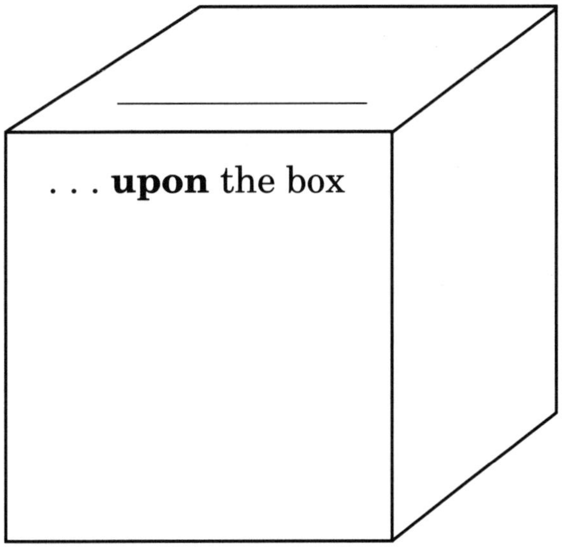

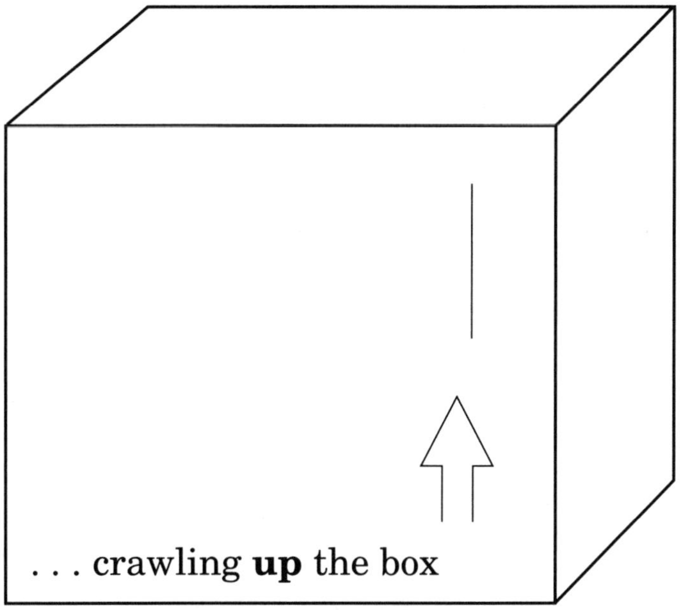

VINES around the VASE

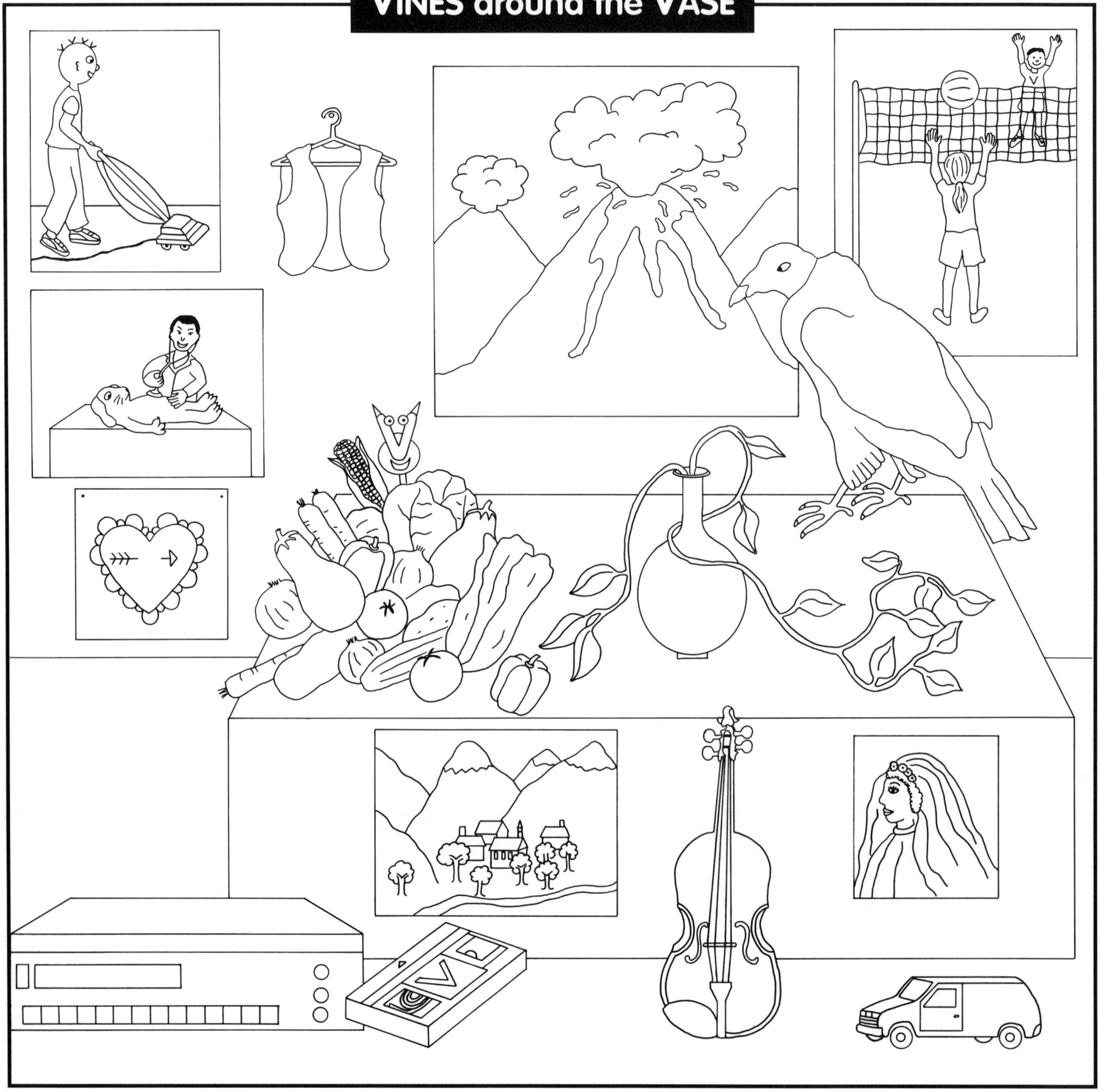

*Look very hard. Do you see the **V** alphabet animal?*

Say the V words and color them.

Put a ✔ by these V words when you find the pictures.

___vase　___vine　___volcano

___violin　___valentine

Vv

More V words that I found:

______
______
______
______
______
______
______
______
______
______
______
______
______
______
______

My V Page

Draw or paste some pictures of **V** words here. Label your pictures.

Vegetables

Circle the **v**egetables that you like.

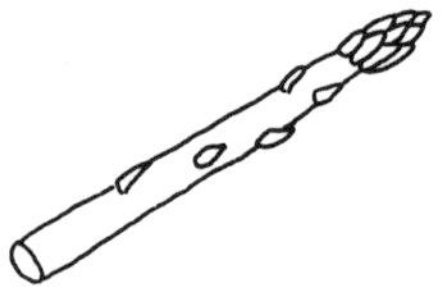

asparagus

beans

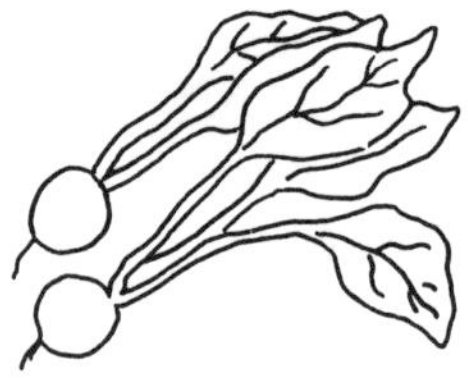

beets

broccoli

cabbage

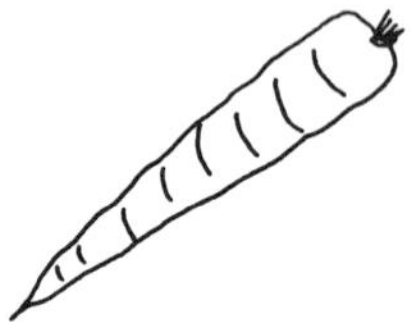

carrot

cauliflower

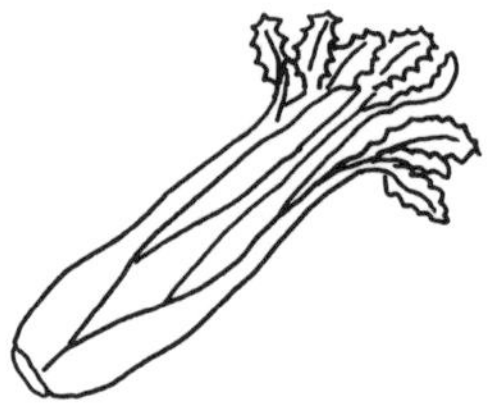

celery

corn

green pepper

lettuce

peas

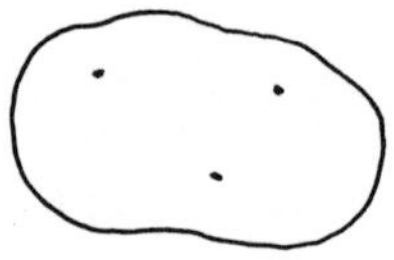

potato

pumpkin

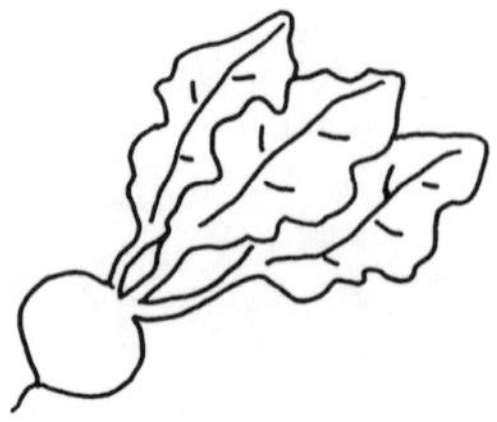

radish

spinach

Draw another **v**egetable here.	Tell about your **v**egetable.
	________________________

Vegetable Soup

Draw your favorite **v**egetables in this soup pot. Add meat and grains for flavor.

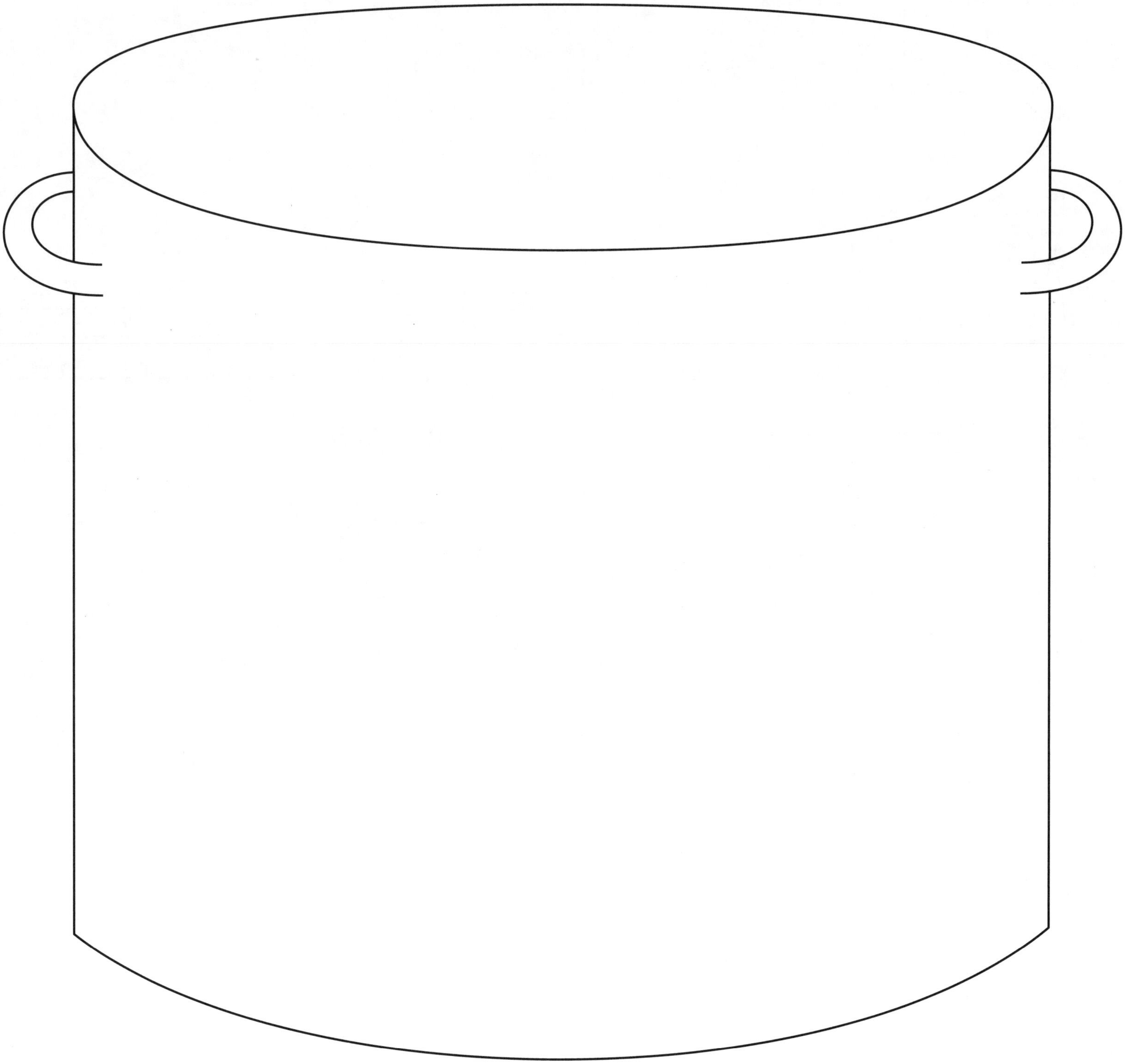

Tell about your **v**egetable soup. ____

____

____

WOLF with a WATERMELON

Where is the **W** *alphabet animal?*

Say the W words and color them.

Put a ✔ by these W words when you find the pictures.

___wagon	___water	___web	___window	___wave
___winter	___watch	___witch	___whale	___write

Ww

More W words that I found:

My W Page

win dow

Draw or paste some pictures of **W** words here. Label your pictures.

Weather Watch

Draw the **w**eather pictures in the boxes above the **w**ords.

windy

rainy / **w**et

warm

sunny

cloudy

snowy

cold /chilly

thunderstorms

lightning

hail

foggy

hot / dry

hazy / humid

Draw a **w**eather picture for each day this **w**eek.

Monday	Tuesday	**W**ednesday	Thursday	Friday	Saturday	Sunday

Write about the **w**eather today. ______________________________

My **W**ish

Make a **w**ish. Draw a picture of your **w**ish.

Write about your **w**ish. ______________________________

____

____

X'S FRONT and CENTER

*Examine the picture for the **X** alphabet animal.*

Say the X words and color them.

Put a ✔ by these front and center X words when you find the pictures.

___**X**-ray ___e**x**it ___ta**x**i

___**x**ylophone ___sa**x**ophone

Xx

More X words that I found:

My X Page

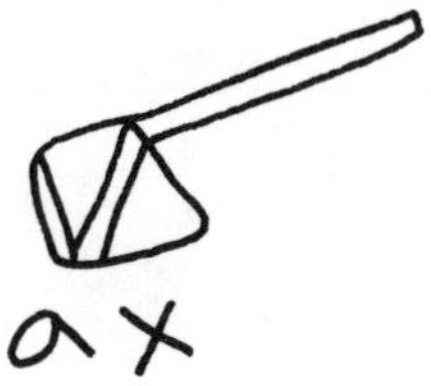

Draw or paste some pictures of **X** words here. Label your pictures.

A YAK and a YACHT

Can you see the **Y** *alphabet animal?*

Say the Y words and color them.

Put a ✔ by these Y words when you find the pictures.

___ yak ___ yo-yo ___ yolk

___ yarn ___ yawn

More Y words that I found:

My Y Page

yarn

Draw or paste some pictures of **Y** words here. Label **y**our pictures.

ZIG ZAG ZIG

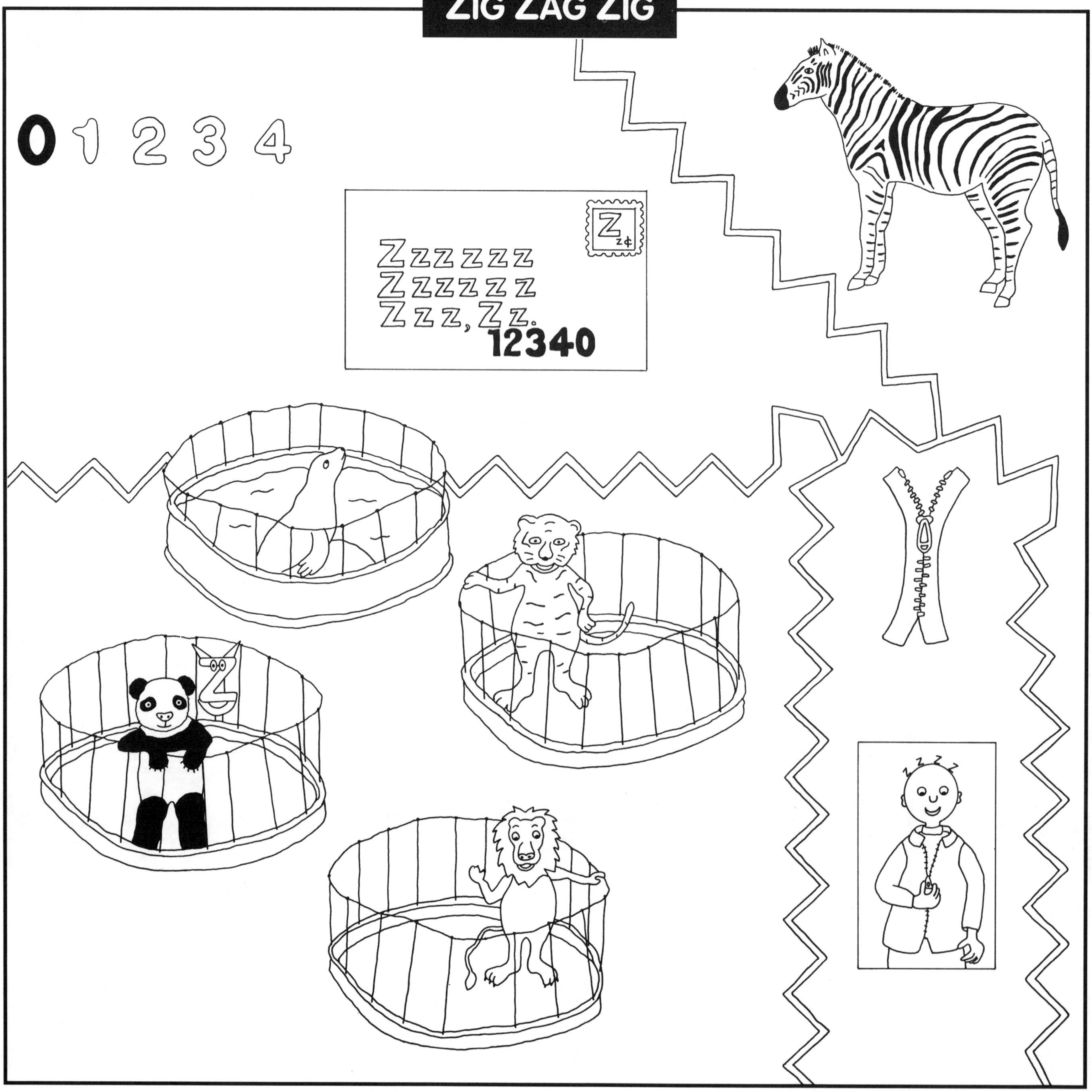

Zero in on the **Z** *alphabet animal.*

Say the Z words and color them.

Put a ✔ by these Z words when you find the pictures.

___zebra ___zero ___zipper

___zoo ___zig-zag

Zz

More Z words that I found:

______

______

______

______

______

______

______

______

______

______

______

______

______

______

______

My Z Page

Draw or paste some pictures of **Z** words here. Label your pictures.

A–Z Review: Verb People

Test yourself. What are the verb people doing? Write an action word under each picture.

(Hint: Look at the letters on their heads.)

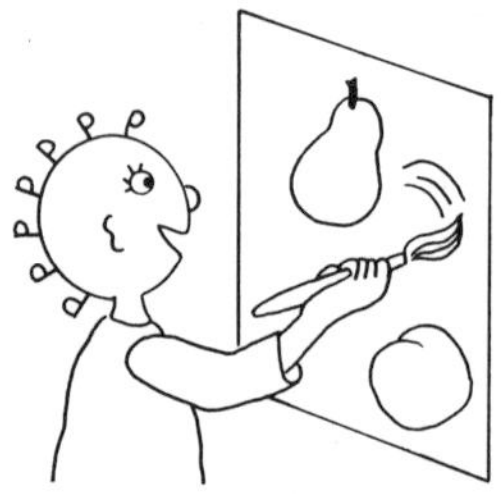

Draw your own verb person doing something **z**any or cra**z**y.

My verb person is ______________________.

How to Use This Book

You will find that students individualize the pages of ***Alligator at the Airport*** in many interesting ways. They are the authors — the creators of the portfolio — and they will define the book. Teachers can be observers and interviewers in this process but should avoid trying to lead too much.

Special Features and Activity Suggestions

1. ***Alphabet scenes.*** Ask students what part of the scene they like best. Why? Is there anything silly or funny? What? Encourage them to describe what they see and tell the story (to practice scanning, naming objects, isolating beginning sounds, explaining, and imagining).

2. ***Verb people.*** Ask students to guess the actions of the verb people (inferring, naming, classifying, practicing initial sounds). The stylized verb figures are included primarily to encourage grammar readiness and challenge older students. You may want to adapt the "A-Z Verb Review" (facing page) for younger students by asking them simply to tell you what the figures are doing.

3. ***Alphabet animals.*** Ask students to describe the location of the alphabet animal in each scene (scanning, referring, using directional words). If partners are working together, they can explain what objects the alphabet animal is behind, beside, between, etc.

4. ***Word lists below the letter scenes.*** Suggest that students try to read words in the caption lists aloud if they can (decoding, analyzing, recognizing, pronouncing). Words in the lists are arranged according to difficulty, with shorter words usually on the first line and longer words on the second line.

5. ***Highlighted letters.*** Ask students if they see the focus letter highlighted anywhere on the activity page (scanning, isolating initial letters, naming). Focus letters are printed in stylized type in the instructions and labels for illustrations. (*X* is the exception, with both "front and center" *x* sounds highlighted.)

6. ***Examples.*** Observe students to see if they understand the examples — words given to start a list or shapes given to suggest scale on a drawing (recognizing, interpreting, inferring). These examples are intended only as guides; some beginning writers may choose to ignore written examples and just do the drawing portion of the page.

7. ***Preposition pages.*** Ask students to explain their drawings on the preposition pages — i.e. Apples around Boxes, Balls by Boxes, Insects in Boxes, etc. (describing, using directional words, practicing vocabulary). You may wish to challenge older students with higher level questions about word usage, but try to avoid the term *preposition* per se with young students; instructions intentionally omit the term in order to keep the activity broad.

8. ***Vocabulary pages.*** Have extra paper on hand for students who wish to expand their lists from the vocabulary pages — i.e. Animals, Clothes, Fruits, Plants, Pets, etc. (naming, labeling, classifying, inferring). These activities are intentionally open-ended so that children will add their own words to each category. Space is provided at the bottom of most vocabulary pages for additions, but inspired writers and artists will need more room.

9. ***Art pages.*** Encourage and enjoy the variety of responses to the art pages (imagining, expressing ideas, visualizing, communicating). These pictures give you a rare glimpse into the minds and lives of your students — their "Dreams," their "Families," their "Holidays," and their "Wishes." Students who are not ready to write full sentences about their pictures may still be able to tell the story aloud or play at writing a few words.

Additional Suggestions for ESL Students

1. ***Labeling.*** Suggest that ESL students label pictures in English whenever they can to improve their written vocabulary.

2. ***Conversation.*** Encourage students to discuss the scenes with classmates or adults to improve their conversational skills. They might start by describing the location of the alphabet animal in the scene or the actions of the verb people.

3. ***Reading aloud.*** Listen as ESL students read their lists of words aloud, and help them improve pronunciation.

4. ***Signature sheet for other listeners.*** You may want to tape a signature sheet inside the back cover so children can have "listeners" sign and indicate pages heard.

5. ***A bilingual dictionary.*** Encourage older students to use a bilingual dictionary to find new words for the lists on their letter pages.

Alligator at the Airport, with your encouragement, can be an artistic adventure for all. Enjoy the creativity. Expand on the ideas. Take off from here.

Dictionary Word List

The page numbers listed here show the first occurrence of each illustrated word. Many of these words appear several more times throughout the book. Words printed in **bold** type also appear in *The Addison-Wesley Picture Dictionary*. Additional high-frequency words are included on activity pages for students to illustrate themselves, for example, *family, holidays,* and *seasons*.